STRATEGIC MANAGEMENT

for
TODAY'S
LIBRARIES

MARILYN
GELL
MASON

American Library Association
Chicago and London
1999

025.1
M41s

Project editor, Bradley Hannan

Cover design by Dianne M. Rooney

Text design and composition by Graphic Composition, Inc., using Meridien and Optima in QuarkXpress 4.0 on a Macintosh platform

Printed on 50-pound white offset, a pH-neutral stock, and bound in 10-point coated cover stock by Data Reproductions

The paper used in this publication meets the minimum requirement of American National Standard for Information Sciences—Permanence of Paper for Printed Library Materials, ANSI Z39.48-1992. ∞

Printed in the United States of America.

03 02 01 00 99   5 4 3 2 1

Contents

Preface   v

Introduction to Strategic Management   1

PART I   **Trend Analysis**   6

1   Trends Challenging the Library:
     Technological, Economic, Social, Political   8
     ALA Yearbook of Library and Information Services, 1985

2   The Future of the Public Library   16
     Library Journal, September 1, 1985

3   The Future Revisited   23
     Library Journal, July 1996

PART II   **Political Context**   28

4   The Politics of Cooperation   31
     Library Journal, November 1, 1973

5   The Politics of Information   37
     Library Journal, September 15, 1979

6   The Fortune Cookie:
     Socio-Political Impact of Information Technology   42
     Special Libraries, spring 1981

7   Washington Update   48
     Library Journal, January 15, March 15, July, December 15, 1981

8   Politics and the Public Library: A Management Guide   55
     Library Journal, March 15, 1989

PART III   **Innovation**   63

9   Managing Innovation   64
     Library Journal, April 1, 1991

Contents

PART IV **Economic Issues**   68

   10 User Fees I: The Economic Argument   69
       Library Journal, January 1, 1979

   11 User Fees II: The Library Response   77
       Library Journal, January 15, 1979

PART V **The Impact of Technology**   83

   12 Library Automation: The Next Wave   85
       Library Administration & Management, v. 5, no. 1, 1991

   13 Sex, Kids, and the Public Library   90
       American Libraries, June/July 1997

   14 Reference Revolutions   93
       Journal of Library Administration, v. 25, no. 2/3, 1998

   15 Educational Programming in the Digital Era   99
       Testimony before the Advisory Committee on Public Interest
       Obligations of Digital Television Broadcasters, January 16, 1988

   16 The Yin and Yang of Knowing   101
       Dædalus, fall 1996

PART VI **Literacy**   108

   17 Libraries, Literacy, and the Future   110
       *Strengthening the Literacy Network: Proceedings of a National
       Forum for State Libraries, May 20–22, 1990*

PART VII **What "Global" Means for Libraries**   114

   18 Is There a Global Role for Metropolitan City Libraries?   115
       American Libraries, September 1994

PART VIII **The Library of Congress**   120

   19 More than a Library *for* Congress: Making LC the Nation's
       Library   121
       Library Journal, November 1, 1993

PART IX **Personal Style**   128

   20 Five Women   129
       Library Journal, November 1, 1975

PART X **Measuring Success**   138

Index   143

Preface

Not long ago, as I was looking through some essays that I had written over the years, I realized that many of the articles that have appeared under my byline in the professional press over the last twenty-five years are, in fact, different aspects of the same topic. That topic is strategic management. Even before strategic management (as something distinct from strategic planning) became a focus of study in businesses and business schools across the country I was fascinated with how an institution, specifically a library, can position itself to take advantage of the broader social, political, economic, and technological trends that provide the context in which it must function.

This volume gathers together the most important of these previously published writings. They are grouped under obvious headings that range from trend analysis to the impact of technology (one of the largest sections) and include sections on political context, innovation, economic issues, and the globalization of library service. I have prefaced each section with a few comments and questions to stimulate discussion.

Several of the articles have played a pivotal role in my personal professional development and make this almost an autobiographical document. The two articles in the economics section led to my being hired as the Director of the White House Conference on Library and Information Services in 1979, and "The Future of the Public Library" brought me to the attention of the Cleveland Public Library Board of Trustees. Others are the culmination of extensive research and thought. My favorites are "Trends for Libraries," originally published in the *ALA Yearbook 1985;* "Politics and the Public Library," published first in *Library Journal;* and "The Yin and Yang of Knowing," an article that first appeared in *Dædalus* but that has been reprinted and written about in the general press. Still others are speeches, published here for the first time.

The first section, on strategic management itself, is new, as is the concluding section on measuring success. Measurement is often thought of as boring and bureaucratic but actually provides us with the vocabulary to communicate with our constituencies. Some might even go so far as to say that if we don't measure it we might as well not do it. But I am getting ahead of myself. First there are the principles of strategic management.

Introduction to Strategic Management

Most management texts describe the functions of management as planning, organizing, staffing, directing, and controlling. Approaches vary, but until quite recently managers and potential managers were instructed in what is now thought of as tactical management, or the ability to manage "down."

While the ability to manage an organization efficiently and effectively to achieve a desired goal is still important, changes in the environment now require those who lead institutions, both public and private, to focus on strategic management, or to manage "out." Most of us now understand that if we manage our resources efficiently and effectively to achieve the wrong goal we have failed. We also understand that if we are moving in the right direction but are unable to find the political and economic support the institution needs, we have also failed. It is not enough to be well organized. The most important jobs for today's managers are to know where the organization is going, attract the necessary support to get there, and motivate staff to make appropriate decisions based not on a set of rules but on a clear understanding of the purpose of the institution.

Strategy and Tactics

One way to think about strategic management is to imagine that you are the captain of a sailboat. Your job is to move the boat from where it is to where you would like it to be, whether that is around the world or across the lake. To achieve that goal you must know where you are, you must decide where you are going, and finally you must chart a course that takes into account the wind, the waves, and the weather that will either help you get there or impede your progress. You must also ensure that you have the appropriate resources for the trip: crew, provisions for the crew, navigational equipment, extra sails, a sound vessel, and so on. This mediation between the boat and the external environment may be thought of as strategic management.

Of course a good captain is also concerned with tactical management. He or she must ensure that the crew is well trained, properly deployed, and that needed specialties are all represented. The captain must make sure that gear is properly stowed and easily available in case of a storm. All crew members must know their jobs and each must be responsible for assigned tasks. Shifts must be established to enable the smooth movement of the boat through the water whatever the conditions. All operations must be well planned, organized, staffed, and controlled. It must be clear to all who is in charge of what. As important as these tasks are, they contribute to the success of the voyage only if the captain is vigilant in monitoring the environment and making course corrections when necessary. A captain who fails this most important responsibility is said to "have his head in the boat," a damning criticism as it exposes the boat and the crew to unexpected dangers.

Organizations have always needed both strategic and tactical management. Today the emphasis has shifted from tactical to strategic management because the environment itself has shifted, is shifting, shifts faster and with less predictability than in those calmer days when the goal remained clearly in sight and resources were comparatively stable. When the weather was good with only an occasional squall, we had the time and could take the time to concentrate on internal management, confident that when we got our head back out of the boat there would be no surprises. Today the weather is rougher and the sea runs fast and high. Staying alert to change is critical.

It has become a cliché to say that change is occurring at an ever increasing rate. Still, change *is* occurring at an ever increasing rate. Computer technology, and the manic speed that drives it, surrounds us and influences everything we come in contact with. We use computers in our libraries, in our homes. They shorten the moment between the event and our perception of the event to such an extent that whole industries are being changed. Stock markets, banking and finance, biotechnology, agribusiness, marketing and advertising, entertainment, everything moves at a fever pitch. Stock prices now respond to news the minute it happens without a pause for analysis; television covers suicide live. Each of us now regularly and routinely juggles e-mail, voice mail, fax, and plain old paper sent with a stamp. We spend so much time talking to our machines that we rarely have time to talk with each other, face to face, in real time. The experience has become so elusive that we have given it a name: face time.

As much as we decry the impact on us individually, we cannot deny or ignore the impact on our institutions. Change is indeed a constant, and the magnitude of that fact emphasizes the need for us to devote more attention to strategic management and more time to monitoring the environment and mediating between it and our libraries.

Strategic Planning

Strategic management had its beginnings in strategic planning, a notion that seems almost quaint today. That is not to say that today's organizations lack a strategic plan. What they lack is strategic planners. Planning today has become everyone's business.

In his seminal article on strategic planning, Henry Mintzberg discusses three reasons for the inadequacy of strategic planning as it is traditionally understood.[1] He calls these the fallacies of strategic planning. They are the fallacy of prediction, the fallacy of detachment, and the fallacy of formalization. The first is a fallacy because the process suggests that "the world is supposed to hold still while a plan is being developed and then stay on the predicted course while that plan is being implemented."

The second assumes that planning and management can be separated in the first place and analyzed in the second. Mintzberg asserts that "innovation has never been institutionalized" and that "strategy making is an immensely complex process, which involves the most sophisticated, subtle, and, at times, subconscious elements of human thinking."

The third fallacy suggests that formal processes can provide a clear road map to the uncharted territory ahead. Strategy making, Mintzberg says, is "a learning process. . . . We think in order to act, to be sure, but we also act in order to think. We try things, and those experiments that work converge gradually into viable patterns that become strategies." He concludes, "This is the very essence of strategy making as a learning process."

In the article and in a subsequent book by the same title, Mintzberg notes that strategic planning is plagued by the speed of change and issues stemming from commitment, politics, and control. We just can't get the world to slow down long enough to plan for the next stage before it is upon us. Strategic planning is an iterative process that must become part of day-to-day management to be effective. In short, to be effective strategic planning must evolve into a much more dynamic form—strategic management.

Functions of Strategic Management

Strategic management is more than planning just as it is more than traditional tactical management. Strategic management implies more than the ability to envision the future. It also includes the ability to implement that vision. In the words of Ian H. Wilson: "It is a continuous process, truly a line-management function that is fundamental to the running of a business—not just planning for it—because it integrates strategy and operations, long-term and short-term, and all functions of the business."[2] If we were to use one word to describe strategic management, that word would be "leadership," because managing change within an institution requires the enthusiastic cooperation of many people both within and outside of it. Leaders are those who are able to get others to follow, to buy in, to believe that an institution can reach its goal. Leaders need followers. We are willing to follow someone only when we believe that he or she is taking us in the right direction with the skill and will to bring us safely through the passage.

Wilson describes the difference between leaders and managers as one of emphasis. Leaders, he says, emphasize the future, emphasize setting direction for "what will be," give vision and inspiration, lead people, build the effectiveness of the organization and emphasize diffused authority. Managers, on the other hand, focus on the present, deal with "what is," execute controls, manage things/programs/resources, focus on organization efficiency, and emphasize chain of command.

If the functions of tactical management are planning, organizing, staffing, directing, and controlling, then the functions of strategic management are *envisioning, planning, communicating,* and *implementing.* While strategic management includes the ability to mobilize on a tactical and operational basis, it also requires the ability to get the external support both politically and financially that is needed to move an institution forward.

Envisioning. Establishing a vision is not the same thing as market analysis. It is also not the same thing as fantasizing. It is a process both rational and intuitive that is based on a careful assessment of the social, economic, political, and technological directions of the broader community. It requires the broadest possible understanding of the underlying mission of the institution. Out of this appreciation for the texture of the future and the role of the library a vision is born that transcends the here and now. Sometimes it comes from a sorting through of data. Sometimes it comes in an intuitive leap. Most often the intuitive leap follows a long period of grappling with sorted and unsorted data.

A visionary sees opportunity where others may only see problems. He or she is skilled at capturing the essence of what is and can be. In business we may think of Bill Gates or Sam Walton, to name only two. In libraries a visionary sees beyond financial constraints and technological challenges. A visionary understands that the goal of the library is to provide information and knowledge, no matter the package, and that a bold plan is more likely to attract needed support than a more timid one. A visionary does not get stuck with lamenting the passing of the way things were and instead embraces the excitement of the way things can be.

This is not to suggest that a vision is abstract or conceptual. If a vision is true and real and achievable, it must be concrete. And it must be exciting. It must have the touch of truth about it. It must engender the "aha" response. "But of course," people will say, "why didn't we think of it before?" No one—not staff, not trustees, not the public or the academic community—no one can support a vision they don't understand. The vision may come in an intuitive leap, but that leap covers the reality of a rapid and accurate assessment of options and opportunities, and it must be explainable. Someone has suggested that the test of what you are doing is your ability to explain it to your grandmother.

Planning. As important as vision is, it takes more than vision to reach a goal. It also takes planning and the ability to implement the plan. Moving from a vision to a plan grounds the project in reality and makes it concrete. In many ways planning takes a vision one step farther. Specific strategic planning provides the road map to move forward, and in putting together the road map we often discover problems that are easier to correct at an early stage.

That is not to say that a plan, no matter how well conceived, becomes rigid, inflexible, and unchanging. A plan sets out a goal, a direction, and interim stops along the way. Since it is based on our understanding of environmental trends and the capabilities of an institution, it is subject to change. A plan tests our understanding of both the institution and the culture in which it exists. These are not static. As change inevitably occurs, we must adapt our plan accordingly. But knowing that it will change does not eliminate the need to plan. Strategic planning, as a subset of strategic management, is a continuing and iterative process. In a sense, the plan is never really completed. It just continues to evolve.

Communicating. The higher up in an organization one rises, the more important communication becomes as a separate, identifiable skill. All the vision in the world won't get you closer to a goal if you are unable to enlist the aid of staff, boards, community leaders, funders, business leaders, the press, the public, friends, and advisors. To be effective it is not only necessary to have an important message, it is also important to tell the story in a way that people are able to hear it. And any good story has a beginning, a middle, and an end.

An effective communicator begins where the interests of the institution and the people who need to support the institution intersect.

An example: if a library is trying to pass a levy for operating support, that message begins at a different point when talking with staff, the editor of the business newspaper, and pastors of local churches. The story may be essentially the same, but a good communicator knows that the beginnings may be quite different in order to capture the attention and establish rapport with the audience—even if the audience is only one person.

Style of delivery is important in other ways as well. A good communicator expresses thoughts cleanly, clearly, often in simple declarative sentences. Metaphors are used to bring the idea home, to relate the unknown of the future to the known of the present. Humor flows easily and appropriately. Communicating a vision requires as much attention as creating the vision in the first place. The communicator, the leader, must connect, if he or she is to be successful in obtaining needed assistance.

Lest we forget, communication also involves listening. The ability to listen is at least as important as the ability to deliver information. When we listen, that is, *really* listen, we learn. We discover ways to improve the vision, the goal. We incorporate the thinking of many people in the formulation of the project and in setting the direction. This strengthens the plan substantively, and it also improves the chances of making it work.

Implementing. Like the image in a Polaroid picture, the detail emerges to fill out the frame. We may have a clear concept of what we thought would show up, but until that photograph is fully developed we won't know if the vision has been realized. The often repeated saying "the devil is in the details" is true. A vision without follow-through is nothing more than a daydream.

It is in the area of implementation that we see more of the tactical and operations functions: organizing, staffing, directing, and controlling. Still, there is a difference. Warren Bennis has observed that "managers catch and ride the waves; leaders create the waves." To use a more specific example, managers might tell you that they can't implement a new program or service because they don't have the needed monies or sometimes the law won't allow it. Leaders, on the other hand, will find new sources of revenue and find ways to change the law.

Integration of functions. The above discussion of the functions of strategic management may sound as if the functions occur sequentially—first you find a vision, then you plan, communicate, and implement. In fact, all of the functions should be going on more or less simultaneously. Vision is developed through experience, and that involves communication, planning, and implementation of other innovations. One does not go off alone to dream up a vision, or a plan, for that matter. The visions for the future arise from the realities of the present. We discuss things with our colleagues, we notice what works and what fails to work; everything, related and unrelated, gets thrown into the pot. Like making a painting or a wonderful meal, strategic management is more art than science. But then today even science is more an art than a science. Even technology, the most practical and rational area of inquiry, depends for change and innovation on careful observa-tion, communication, experimentation, and an intuitive leap.

Conclusion

Many of our most successful leaders practice strategic management intuitively. They understand change and the requirements of change. They know that if libraries are to survive and thrive they must be an integral part of their community, whether that is a public, a private, or an academic community. In each environment, a leader looks to the future, for whoever heard of leadership into the past? Leaders understand the forces that bring change; they assess options; they plan, they communicate, and most important of all, leaders have a bias toward action. It is these characteristics that are the hallmarks of strategic management. It is these characteristics that mark a leader.

NOTES

1. Henry Mintzberg (1994), "The Rise and Fall of Strategic Planning," *Harvard Business Review* 72 (January/February), 107-14.

2. Ian H. Wilson (1996), "The Five Compasses of Strategic Leadership," *Strategy and Leadership* 24, no. 4 (July-August), 26-32.

PART I

Trend Analysis

Trend analysis should not be confused with futuristic crystal ball gazing, in spite of the fact that several of the articles that follow contain the word "future" in the title. It is not an attempt to predict precisely what will occur at a specific point in the future as much as it is a process that enables us to understand overarching forces that are likely to have an impact on all our institutions. It is, in the words of the first article, "Trends Challenging the Library," "largely a matter of selection. What we choose to focus our attention on will condition our judgments about the best set of strategies for the development of our libraries."

The first article focuses on four areas: technological, economic, social, and political change. While specific facts in each of these areas have changed, as one would expect, I was struck by the fact that the trends described are not significantly different in their impact today than they were when the article was written in 1985.

Computers today "continue to become smaller, faster, cheaper, more reliable, and more pervasive." The fact that the entire contents of the Library of Congress can now fit on a disc that would fit in a shirt pocket rather than on two hundred feet of shelving merely serves to emphasize the ongoing dynamic of technological change.

In the area of economic change, the move toward an international economy has accelerated, as everyone knows, and this trend is nowhere more apparent than in the publishing industry. Mergers and takeovers have become an international pastime, as many now wonder aloud whether the information revolution is promoting or inhibiting diverse points of view. Scholarly publishing, especially, is beginning to be viewed by scholars themselves as an inhibiting force, a topic that is addressed later in this book.

Literacy has continued to plummet. Fewer people read less and less as icons appear to have usurped the landscape that was once marked by the printed word. Some claim that technology will help overcome the literacy gap, while others appear to have given up altogether. And while the Gramm-Rudman-Hollings amendment has become a footnote in congressional history, the major concerns about the appropriate role of the federal government remain the same, and the observation that "some additional reduction of federal support for social services is almost inevitable" has proved to be all too true.

There is nothing magical about the topic choices of technological, economic, social, and political change. Other areas are equally ripe for analysis. Legal issues, especially regarding copyright, merit extended and close scrutiny. Movement of our population between urban and suburban cultures also has an important impact on libraries. As you read through this section you might want to ask yourself questions like these:

- Amidst all the change, how do you decide what elements are most likely to impact libraries?
- What would you identify as the most important trends today?
- Can you extrapolate from the past and the present into the future, or do some things snap into a completely different reality?
- Can you give some examples of predictable change and unpredictable change?

Trend analysis is important because it helps us understand libraries in a broader context. In the final analysis, however, a trend implies direction, not destination. Destiny is determined by choices. The environment in which we live and work is complex, contradictory, and exciting. The planning that we do depends not only on our understanding of trends but also on our interpretation and selection of options and opportunities.

1

Trends Challenging the Library: Technological, Economic, Social, Political

The Future in Retrospect

At a December retreat of the OCLC Board of Trustees, Larry Roberts stunned trustees and staff alike by announcing that three Japanese firms are now marketing a device that allows an IBM PC to handle compact disks. The device has a read/write capability as opposed to the familiar read-only format, and one disk holds 2.4 gigabytes of information using both sides. That level of data compression means that one million pages of text in digital form can be stored on a single side of a compact disk. In optical, or scanned storage (which preserves diagrams, layout, and other materials) one side of a disk will hold 36,000 pages. The largest disk previously available has one-fifth that capacity. The device costs $3,000; the read/write disk is $20.

In 1985, corporate America participated in the largest spate of mergers, acquisitions, and takeovers in history. Companies acquired other companies at the astonishing rate of eleven a day with the total value of these deals expected to exceed the record of $125 billion reached in 1984. *Time* quoted Democratic Representative Timothy Wirth, who chairs a House subcommittee that has been studying acquisitions, as saying: "These mergers and takeovers are having as profound an impact on the American economy as the advent of the great railroads, the airplane and the telephone."

Jonathan Kozol shocked many in 1985 by reporting in his passionate book *Illiterate America* that one-third of the entire adult population of the United States is functionally illiterate. In more specific terms, twenty-five million Americans read so poorly that they are unable to read the poison warnings on a can of pesticide, a note from a child's teacher, or the front page of a newspaper. Moreover, the problem is growing at an alarming rate. In just fourteen years the number of identified nonreaders has tripled.

In what House Majority Leader Jim Wright characterized as "an act of legislative desperation," Congress ended the first session of the Ninety-ninth Congress by passing a piece of legislation that will most likely recast the role of the federal government. The Balanced Budget and Emergency Deficit Control Act of 1985 (the Gramm-Rudman-Hollings amendment), known informally as Gramm-Rudman, was signed into law by President Reagan on December 12. It requires the federal government to balance its budget over six years through a process of "sequestering," or impoundment of funds. Seventy-three percent of the federal budget has been exempted from the cuts, leaving 27 percent of federal programs to absorb funding reductions.

Reprinted from the *ALA Yearbook of Library and Information Services, 1985*

Strategic planning for an institution requires an assessment of environmental trends and their potential impact on the institution in question. Each of the paragraphs above describes one version of the future, or at least one view of factors that are seen as critical to the shaping of a future. Obviously where one stands with respect to the most likely unfolding of events depends on where one sits in relation to these and other developments in our society. Forecasting is therefore largely a matter of selection. What we choose to focus our attention on will condition our judgments about the best set of strategies for the development of our libraries.

I have chosen the conventional areas of social, political, economic, and technological change as the most appropriate spheres for inquiry. In each I have identified trends that are most likely to have the greatest impact on libraries over the next five to fifteen years. Clearly it is not a comprehensive list. I have avoided including an analysis of the potential for cataclysmic change, choosing instead to assume a reasonably stable environment in which current trends, if unchecked, will move toward more or less natural conclusions.

Technological Change

Technological change is the easiest to describe and possibly the most difficult to interpret. Easily measured, fast-moving computer and communications developments have provided the basis for what has become known as the Information Age. The fact that computers continue to become smaller, faster, cheaper, more reliable, and more pervasive is obvious and even expected.

In the early 1950s it would have taken a computer the size of New York City, and drawing more power than the subway system, to perform the functions now available on a personal computer. This compression in size is a direct result of the development of the transistor and the subsequent miniaturization and integration possible on a silicon chip.

By 1980, 100,000 transistors (capable of storing 100,000 bits of information) could be integrated on a single piece of silicon one quarter-inch square. Today, IBM has developed and is testing a chip that contains 1,000,000 bits of information. Some scientists anticipate the ultimate creation of a 30,000,000-bit chip.

Laser disk technology offers an increasingly attractive high density storage option. Using this technology, it is now possible to store the entire contents of the Library of Congress on disks that would fit on two hundred feet of shelving, or on one wall of a large room. Moreover, scanning techniques that can convert print material to disk storage are progressing rapidly. Equipment now exists that will scan at the rate of eight pages per minute. By the end of 1986, the rate is expected to increase to twelve pages per minute. The cost to reproduce a disk after creation of the initial master (which can contain the full text of over two hundred volumes) is less than $20 per disk. Industry watchers predict that laser disk publishing and information distribution will be a $2 billion to $4 billion industry by 1990.

Online databases continue to provide access to specialized information of all types. The number of publicly available databases rose from 500 in 1980 to 2,600 in 1985. Moreover, detailed 1980 census information is available only in this format. Some experts predict that 25 percent of the information now contained in reference books will be offered only in machine-readable form by 1990.

As information itself proliferates and becomes available in a variety of formats, access to machine-readable information is also expanding. A 1983 study by International Data Corporation revealed that among white collar workers the 1983 ratio of computer to worker was one to three. By 1987, however, that ratio is expected to be one to one, creating an environment in which literally every office worker will have access to either a personal computer or computer terminal.

While computer developments have progressed generally as expected, communications technologies have in some instances failed to live up to their earlier promise. Cable is not as widespread as many in the industry had hoped and is used primarily to improve the quality of the television signal and to provide access to certain "premium" entertainment channels. Its use for the transmission of more serious information has not materialized. Viewdata and teletext systems remain experimental as use of the cable for data transmission appears to be more expensive than use of telephone lines.

Satellites continue to play an important role in international communications. In addition, there are now 400,000 privately owned satellite dishes in the United States and there is some indication that their existence is cutting sharply into the cable market. The use of satellite dishes is growing at the rate of 300 percent a year. While some experts expect that rate to continue as satellite dishes become about the size of a salad bowl, there is considerable activity on the regulatory front as cablecasters and others look for ways to limit the ability of individuals to pull down signals. It is unclear how these issues, which are more political than technical, will be resolved.

The most important development in the area of communications has been the change in rate structures that followed deregulation of AT&T. Increased competition in long distance service has been offset by the increased cost of local service, as many predicted. In general, rising communication costs have been the greatest limitation on the use of remotely held databases.

In this context the announcement of a read/write disk has special significance. It provides a mechanism by which the impact of costly communications can be minimized. Consider the implications for a service like Dialog. To use Dialog databases now, a user must dial up the computer and search online. Costs include not only access charges but communications charges as well. If, however, Dialog published its databases on read/write laser disks, the disks could be sold to users and updated as frequently as the user wished. To update the information a user would simply dial up during off-peak hours and use high-speed transmission to receive any changes that had been made. At the same time Dialog would no doubt require the user to send usage information. Obviously, a variety of pricing mechanisms are possible.

The technology described above is available today. None of it is futuristic. In the years ahead we are sure to see greater use and more imaginative application of these technologies. But the technological trend line is clear: greater access to more information. Other trends in the use of computer technology are not so clear. These include: the increased use of computer chips in everything from dolls to dishwashers, the development and use of robotics, and the development of fifth-generation computer systems.

Robotics has been heralded as the key to the second industrial revolution. Indeed, such machines, equipped with computerized functions, may help the United States regain a leadership position in world trade. Already there are 37,000 robots at work in the United States. This number is expected to grow to 350,000 within the next five years as U.S. firms invest $300 million to $500 million to automate industrial production. Although the use of robots to perform dangerous or demeaning tasks is appealing, the impact on the U.S. labor force cannot be estimated at this time.

If robotics is expected to bring about the second industrial revolution, fifth-generation computers are expected to introduce the second computer revolution. Fifth-generation computers will be characterized by the ability to handle huge amounts of information; communicate using everyday language, jargon, or symbols; apply the functions of learning, associating, and inferring; and package information to meet the specific needs of an individual. In short, fifth-generation computers will merge artificial intelligence functions with an enormous storage and processing capability.

As ambitious as such a computer may sound, four major fifth-generation projects are now under way. They are the Japanese Knowledge Information Processing Systems (KIPS) group; the Alvey Programme of the United Kingdom's Department of Industry; the European Strategic Programme for Research in Information Technology (ESPRIT); and the Microelectronics and Computer Technology Corporation (MCC) in the United States.

Confident that fifth-generation computers are the wave of the future, Fred Kilgour and two colleagues at OCLC have already begun to develop a prototype system which could become the model for the library of the future. The Electronic Information Delivery Online System (EIDOS) when operational will enable the user to search through full texts of monographs and retrieve needed information. It relies on electronic publishing and easy access to microcomputers, trends which are proceeding rapidly and independently.

The promise of technology is often oversold. There was a time when many felt that the Information Age would provide us with a communications/transportation trade-off. As it happens, increased communications appears to stimulate travel, not reduce it. Many libraries, and many vendors, continue to struggle with automating circulation control and other internal library functions. Nevertheless, the library profession has used computers to make significant progress in some areas. Cataloging is faster and far less costly than it was in the days before OCLC was introduced and many reference librarians now rely on database searches to provide more up-to-date information in less time.

Whatever we may think of the technology, it is a force that conditions our environment. Its impact will continue and is likely to accelerate. This is true not only because of the nature of the technology itself but also because of the changing economics of the information industry.

Economic Change

The information industry, which affects libraries far more than we like to admit, has been a part of the merger phenomenon de-scribed earlier. In 1985 International Thomson acquired Carrolton Press and UTLAS, which subsequently acquired the ALIS III system from DataPhase; TBG (formerly Thyssen-Bornemisza NV.) took over BRS, Predicasts, Information Handling Services, and CLSI; and OCLC, the U.S. entry in the international information sweepstakes, began to expand both its product line and market as it developed cooperative ventures with libraries in Europe and Asia.

With a revenue stream of $2 billion a year, International Thomson Organisation, a British firm, is the big kid on the block. Through its companies and subsidiaries International Thomson publishes primary and reference materials, including both monographs and periodicals, and now, with its acquisition of Carrolton and UTLAS, offers specialized information services. Ten of its companies and subsidiaries in the United States alone (they include Derwent, Gale Research, Thomson and Thomson, and Carrolton) offer more than twenty-six different databases in a variety of fields. International Thomson plans to become a "full service" information organization through acquisition of existing companies and development of needed products. Its strong financial position makes the achievement of such an ambitious goal likely.

TBG, a Dutch firm, is only slightly smaller than International Thomson. Its revenue stream is approximately $1.7 billion a year. Like Thomson, TBG appears to have targeted the U.S. market for both acquisitions and sales. Unlike Thomson, however, TBG appears to be looking beyond the library market. Nevertheless, a possible integration of BRS services with CLSI systems would be a very powerful offering to the library world. Moreover, the scope of CLSI installations provides a broad existing client base.

Although OCLC, an American, not-for-profit corporation, is usually thought of as the giant of U.S. information organizations, its revenue stream of less than $100 million per year puts it at a disadvantage when compared with the companies described here. While OCLC has been expanding both its base of operations (Europe and Asia) and its product line (LS 2000 is one example), it continues to generate most of its revenue from use of its database for cataloging and related functions. There is some irony in the fact that the United States, which is generally thought of as the preeminent capitalist country, is represented in the world information arena by a cooperative membership organization.

Other companies that have an important impact on the library environment have also been busy merging and acquiring. Bell & Howell announced its intent to buy UMI from Xerox and the Image-processing Systems Division of S.T.C. Canada, Inc. Dun & Bradstreet, which already provides credit service and publishes the electronic version of the official Airline Guide as well as providing the more familiar business-oriented information services, bought Datastream PLC, London.

Elsevier, a printing and publishing business based in Amsterdam and known primarily for its scientific publications, also owns Congressional Information Services; Excerpta Medica, Online; Elsevier Science Publishers; Greenwood Press; and Medical Examination Publishing. Pergamon Group of London, which includes Pergamon Press and Pergamon-InfoLine, acquired Information on Demand in 1983.

Reed International is a holding company active in the United Kingdom, North America, and continental Europe. Reed Holdings, Inc., a wholly owned subsidiary, recently acquired R. R. Bowker from Xerox. Ziff, a privately held company, owns several computer publications and five information companies. One of its companies, Information Access Corporation, acquired Harfax Database Publishing from Harper & Row in 1984.

These corporate developments are important to libraries because libraries are dependent on corporate suppliers to operate and also because this trend embodies many of the elements that are shaping the environment. There is a clear move toward an increasingly international economy. This is true for the economy as a whole and it is specifically true for information based companies and li-

braries. The importance of electronic publishing is growing. The technology described above is generating new business opportunities for those in the information industry and new choices for libraries. Finally, the need for adequate capitalization for product development is finally being met as larger corporations enter the information market. Those libraries that have struggled with inadequately capitalized firms that have promised more than they can afford to deliver may welcome this change.

Libraries appear to be moving toward an environment with fewer, larger vendors. While many will try to provide virtually all the products and services a library may need, a more likely development, at least in the library automation field, is the component approach. Instead of buying a "turnkey" system, more libraries will put together their own systems with pieces offered by different vendors in much the same way that an individual may put together a stereo system.

A look at all parts of the economy finds a trend toward blending, consolidation, the formation of associations, the development of cooperative or joint projects. Maturing computer and communications technologies are creating an environment in which new combinations are not only possible, they are unavoidable. Many of the acquisitions an mergers described here are designed to take advantage of that environment. They promise a greater variety of information available in a vast array of formats. Instead of creating a kind of monolithic society, this trend toward aggregation is creating, at least for the next decade, greater variety that is more widely distributed. New unions are creating greater choice.

Social Change

Unfortunately, not everyone in North American society enjoys the fruits of the Information Age. The United States has become a divided country with economic opportunity on the one side and institutionalized poverty on the other; a nation with political representation for some and disenfranchisement for others; a nation where many have access to more information than they can use and others cannot read. The United States is a nation that counsels its people to lift themselves up by the bootstraps of learning but fails to provide the boots of literacy.

There are many ways to describe the trends of social change. We are growing older, as the baby boomers become yuppies on their way to social security. The population is shifting south, giving cities like Houston and Los Angeles an opportunity to struggle with the problems of Philadelphia and New York. Cities throughout the country are renewing themselves in creative and productive ways, some more successfully than others. Our families are smaller, with more single person households, more single parent families, and more families in which both parents work. All of these characteristics have implications for service provided by our nation's libraries. But nothing—no force, no trend—is having quite as subversive an impact as the plague of illiteracy.

According to Jonathan Kozol, illiteracy afflicts one-third of the adult population. Twenty-five million Americans read not at all or below the fifth-grade level. Another thirty-five million read below the ninth-grade level. Altogether sixty million adults are unable to hold any but the most menial of jobs.

On a practical level 26 percent of adult Americans, given a paycheck and stub listing deductions, cannot tell if their paycheck is correct. Thirty-six percent are unable to list the right number of exemptions on a W-4 form. Forty-four percent cannot match their qualifications with job requirements listed in help wanted ads. Twenty-two percent cannot address an envelope well enough to get it to its destination while 24 percent cannot supply their correct return address. Over 20 percent are unable to write a check that a bank can process.

One-third of our nation's adults get information only from television, the radio, or through friends and associates. About 45 percent of American adults do not read newspapers, with only 10 percent abstaining by choice. As a result, newspapers, the free press guaranteed by our Constitution, are having a difficult time surviving. Books, too, are read by an ever diminishing portion of the population. An alarming 40 percent of adults under twenty-one years of age do not read books at all. Given such limited access to information, sixty million Americans are excluded from the political process. Political decisions, when they are made at all, are made on the basis of limited, superficial information.

The costs of this national disgrace are appalling. In human terms, options are so limited that choice is a delusion. A nation unwilling to support effective education for children and appropriate literacy training programs for adults finds itself paying in other ways. One study estimates direct out-of-pocket costs to business and taxpayers at $20 billion a year. Lost revenue resulting from unemployment or underemployment would raise that number significantly. Direct costs include $6 billion in child welfare payments and unemployment compensation caused directly by the inability to perform tasks for which employment is available. The cost is $6.6 billion to support prison inmates whose incarceration is directly linked to illiteracy. Court costs and workers' compensation also contribute to the total, while health expenditures linked to the inability to read go unestimated.

If this trend continues it is sure to have a dramatic impact on libraries. An illiterate population is not likely to see any need to support an institution whose very existence is a challenge. No matter how much libraries invest in nonprint material, books, periodicals, and their equivalent in electronic format remain the staple of our existence. Given the economy and efficiency of the written word, there is no evidence that we are likely to see that situation change in the foreseeable future.

Political Change

It seems unlikely that help will come from Washington, where there is a clear trend toward a decreased federal role in the provision of all sorts of services, especially social services. The Gramm-Rudman-Hollings amendment is the most recent and sweeping measure to come before the Congress. Gramm-Rudman itself came as something of a surprise. It was introduced as an amendment to debt ceiling extension legislation that is usually passed each year. In addition, it appeared without hearings and with little advance notice. Nevertheless, it struck a responsive chord among members of Congress who were growing restless with the ever increasing national debt.

One reason the bill is appealing is that it calls for automatic cuts through a process of sequestering or impoundment should the president and Congress be unable to agree on cuts that would meet the targeted reduction amount. The very fact that the national debt has ballooned so dramatically over the last five years in spite of rhetoric on all sides calling for a balanced budget suggests that such agreement is unlikely.

The primary problem with the legislation is that domestic discretionary programs (the 27 percent of the federal budget not exempt from cuts) would bear the brunt of the reductions. Initial estimates place program cuts for FY '86 at 4.6 percent with cuts for FY '87 in the 30 percent range. Cuts in domestic programs beyond the third year are staggering and most observers feel that some tax increase is inevitable. Projections are still preliminary and are complicated by several lawsuits challenging various provisions of the act and now pending before the Supreme Court. The loss of general revenue-sharing monies is affecting the ability of local and state governments to continue to fund programs at even the existing level.

Whatever happens with Gramm-Rudman, the concern about mounting federal debt will continue, as will an aversion to major tax increases. Some additional reduction of federal support for social services is almost inevitable. (Domestic discretionary spending has already been cut 34 percent over five years.) Although the specific impact on library programs is still unclear, a reduction in federal grants-in-aid to public, academic, and school libraries will have a profound effect on state library agencies and state and regional networks as well, thereby shaking the entire infrastructure that has been established for library development and resource sharing.

Given this general trend and its likely outcome, it may be time for the library profession to begin to rethink the appropriate roles of various levels of government in supporting libraries. Most of the federal grants-in-aid programs were developed in the 1960s. Although amended from time to time, they have not been significantly restructured. Since then the environment in which libraries function has changed markedly. Networks have been born (and some have died), technology has created new challenges and opportunities, and major resource libraries face mounting economic pressures. Perhaps librarians should begin to define the role of the federal government more sharply and develop new strategies for securing additional state and local support.

Impact on Libraries

The technological, economic, social, and political trends described here have some general themes in common. They all point to a time of changing roles and relationships, of increased independence and interdependence (not mutually exclusive concepts), of greater participation in worldwide sharing of information, and of increased concern for the individual.

Information technology is offering alternatives that were previously unavailable. As functions change, forms will follow. Old, revered distinctions as basic as the differences among public, school, academic, and special libraries are likely to disappear. Those who feel that this is an overstatement might contemplate the already fuzzy lines that separate networks from vendors on the one hand and large library systems on the other.

Technology has bent the straight line that previously held independence at one end and interdependence at the other into a circle, bringing the two together. Through networks of associations with other libraries and other institutions, an individual library can now offer more to its user. As the packaging and repackaging of information continues at the national and international levels this trend will accelerate.

A worldwide information community is developing with the emergence of large international information companies and the computer and communications capabilities needed for rapid transfer of information. Still, the library focus will continue to be the individual user. The technology that makes it possible to collect, store, and distribute huge amounts of information will also enable libraries to tailor services designed quite specifically for an individual.

But there is a darker side to the future. Illiteracy stalks the nation, threatening the very fabric of society, and the federal government appears to be abandoning its commitment to social programs. These trends are disquieting and disruptive. They stand in marked contrast to the more positive indications of growth and development.

In the final analysis, however, a trend implies direction, not destination. Destiny is determined by choices. The environment in which we live and work is complex, contradictory, and exciting. The planning that we do depends not only on our understanding of trends but also on our interpretation and selection of options and opportunities.

2

The Future of the Public Library

If men learn this, it will implant forgetfulness in their souls; they will cease to exercise memory because they rely on that which is written, calling things to remembrance no longer from within themselves, but by means of external marks. What you have discovered is a recipe not for memory but for reminder. And it is not true wisdom that you offer disciples, but only its semblance, for by telling them of many things without teaching them you will make them seem to know much, while for the most part they know nothing, and as men filled, not with wisdom, but with the conceit of wisdom, they will be a burden to their fellows.

—Plato, *Dialogues*, Phaedrus

Plato was not the first to be suspicious of modern technology and he certainly has not been the last. For Plato, writing appeared dangerous. It offered information without discourse and so threatened the established order. While there is a fine irony in the fact that Plato chose to express his concerns in the very form he condemned, the suspicion and threat were real. Writing did in fact undermine discourse as it extended human memory and changed forever the face of the world.

Today's technology is no less threatening. Computers with their dazzling speed and impressive storage capacity appear to offer an alternative to the printed word. Libraries were founded on the written word and print has

dominated our institutions for centuries. Thus we react with varying degrees of skepticism to claims currently being made for future applications of computers.

Few librarians see computers as the panacea for all that ails their institutions. Some of the more honest among us are straightforward in asking what these machines will do to our jobs. Will librarians be needed in the brave new world described by the technologically enthusiastic? What about libraries themselves? Will they have a role when the entire contents of the Library of Congress can be reduced to optical disk and stored on twenty feet of shelving?

Instead of addressing these issues head on, many of us have embarked on a voyage of economic discovery. Using terms like "public good," "externality," and "spillover," we have struggled to justify what we do on the basis of a value system few of us accept. Nevertheless we persist because economic concepts offer us a way to control technological change.

Libraries as Competitors

Consider fees. Fees were never an issue when we were talking about fines for overdue books. They became an issue only when libraries began to charge for computer searches. Alternatively, few raised the specter of unfair competition with the private sector when the private sector in question was the corner bookstore. Libraries have always competed with booksellers, just as public schools compete with private schools, public health facilities compete with private medical care, and private security services compete with and supplement publicly supported police departments. To suggest that easy and clear distinctions can be made is preposterous. Nevertheless, as some libraries prepare to establish fee-based information retrieval services some voices cry foul and frequently go on to suggest that the need for public libraries has past.

Technology is bringing about an order of magnitude change. To put it bluntly, the stakes are higher, much higher. Because technology offers powerful new tools, libraries are both threatened and threatening, depending on your point of view. Economic arguments provide a justification for keeping the technology, and the library, in its place. At the same time, however, these economic preoccupations have obscured the real questions, which are neither economic nor technological. The real questions are ones of purpose and value.

The Purpose of the Library

The purpose of the public library remains unchanged. In this country it is to support a democratic form of government through public access to information and knowledge. More generally, materials found in libraries provide challenge, perspective, comfort, assistance, opportunity, relief, and access to information, to knowledge, and to change. Libraries are learning institutions. They provide an individual with the resources necessary to understand the past, cope with the present, and plan for the future. They nourish the mind, stimulate the spirit, and provide a means of escape from the shackles of ignorance. If public libraries did not exist they would have to be invented, for a democratic form of government without access to information necessary for decision making is unthinkable.

The critical issue is not what libraries should do, but how they can best accomplish their mission in a highly technological environment.

The Forecasts

The following forecasts are predictions about the future of the public library. They are not exhaustive in scope but are limited to the kinds of change we can expect if technological trends, economic constraints, and political conditions continue as some variation of the present without a major break or cataclysmic change.

The forecasts are based on an analysis of available data, the assumption that technology offers some important opportunities, and an abiding confidence in the elasticity of our public libraries.

Finally, they reflect specific experiences and long-range plans for the Atlanta-Fulton Public Library. This author is tired of hearing about the impending death of the public library and believes that very often our assets and our liabilities are really the same, opposite sides of the same coin. It is not necessarily the situation that must change, it may be only the direction from which we view the coin.

Forecast 1

The public library of the future will be judged not by the size of its collections, but by its success in providing information quickly and accurately.

This prediction is based on a continuation of current trends. Each year most libraries purchase a smaller percentage of published materials than they did the year before. This has been the result of the increased cost of books and other materials, an increased production from publishers, and static or reduced library budgets. In the area of journal publication alone, studies indicate that approximately 120,000 titles are now published worldwide on an annual basis. Most public libraries purchase less than one percent of these.

Libraries have responded to this situation by forming and participating in networks and cooperatives. Aided by computer and communications technologies, OCLC, AMIGOS, SOLINET, and other regional and local networks have facilitated interlibrary loan. Interlibrary loan traffic in periodical material alone is expected to reach twenty million items in 1985.

Although the current system is expensive, cumbersome, time consuming, and frustrating for both librarians and library users, the trend toward increased sharing of materials is certain to continue. As the time between the request for material and delivery of an item is shortened by improved communications technologies (such as new and cheaper forms of facsimile transmission), this trend will accelerate.

One element often overlooked in discussions of library service is the value of currency in the information we provide. This is true whether we are talking about providing the latest best-seller while it is still a best-seller, up-to-date statistical information, or stock market quotations. Students, businesses, and curious people want prompt answers to their questions. That is one reason why researchers and others have tended to use libraries with large collections in the past. They were more likely to find what they needed without waiting.

With greater distribution of printed material, increased use of optical disk and other compact storage techniques, emergence of publication on demand, and proliferation of electronic databases (there are now over 2,400, many of them full text), libraries without large collections will be able to provide prompt access to materials and quick answers to questions.

Forecast 2

Within ten years over half of the service provided to library users will be to individuals who never come into the library.

A recent study conducted by Robert M. Mason and Georgia Tech revealed that by 1990 more than 90 percent of office workers will have access to either a computer terminal or a microcomputer. Even more astonishing, 25 percent of the information now contained in reference books is expected to be offered only in machine-readable form by 1990, and by the year 2000, 25 percent of existing journals will be published and made available exclusively in electronic form.

Already public libraries are relying heavily on that time-honored communications device called the telephone to answer reference questions. In Atlanta, Information Line is our most popular and cost-effective service. It is, in fact, saturated to the point that we have no idea what the demand would be if we could begin to meet it. As these telephone reference services expand, as they most certainly will in Atlanta, it is only a short step to a more exotic scenario.

Within ten years it is entirely possible that a public library will be able to help a citizen identify a document located in Tokyo, have it sent via satellite, and transmit it to the individual's home or office using telephone lines or cable and facsimile equipment. In even fewer years we will be able to provide search services whereby a librarian may research a question using printed materials and/or databases as appropriate, download or reproduce the material needed, and send it out immediately by mail, courier, or electronic transmission depending on the needs of the patron and the bulk of the material.

Forecast 3

Public libraries will develop an information infrastructure to provide access to a growing and changing flow of information.

In urban planning the word infrastructure is usually used to describe that system of roads, water, sewer, and other basic services that are necessary for the development and use of land. The term information infrastructure is used here in an analogous manner. It includes communications channels, delivery systems, and access points needed for the development and use of information.

Communications channels consist of telephone lines, cable, and satellite transmission. Delivery systems may be U.S. mail, facsimile transmission, courier, electronic transmission, and probably a few not thought of or not invented. Primary access points will be home, office, and branch library.

Information contained in print or electronic form may change, but the infrastructure will be able to accommodate a growing, changing flow. As public libraries shift their emphasis from a place orientation to a service orientation, connections between existing service units will be strengthened and the importance of the pipeline will be emphasized.

Forecast 4

This infrastructure will include more, smaller library branches.

Most communities will find the need for more, not fewer, branches, reversing the trend of the last thirty years. Justification for the construction of more, smaller branches can be found in demographic trends, emerging patterns of library usage, and technological developments.

Demographically we have become a nation of single-person households, single-parent families, and families in which both parents work full time. Family units composed of two resident parents, one of which serves as a chauffeur every afternoon, and two or three children have largely disappeared.

Because of these changes, most of us, and most of our users, are constantly pressed for time. We use services that are close to home and easy to use. The neighborhood library, accessible to many on foot or by public transportation, is growing in importance. This importance will be further enhanced as we put communications systems in place that will make it possible for every branch library to provide sophisticated information services using information technology.

When information was largely contained in books it made sense to build fewer, larger branches simply because many volumes were needed to provide a critical mass of information and duplication was costly. With the growing capabilities of computer and communications technologies, the public library of the future will be able to centralize its specialized materials and services while seeking wide distribution of neighborhood libraries. These branches will become access points to a larger, sophisticated information system while continuing to provide the materials and services required by the individual neighborhood.

Librarians have long discussed the plight of the information poor in an information-rich world. Neighborhood libraries can help assure continued access to a range of information for everyone regardless of income level or technological sophistication. The neighborhood library of the future (like today's neighborhood library) will be small, an integral part of the neighborhood, sensitive to the information needs of the immediate community, and a comfortable, friendly place to be.

In addition, however, it will provide access to a huge range of information and services by using computer and communications technologies and efficient delivery systems. It will be an access point for those who do not have computers or computer terminals in their homes or offices.

Forecast 5

Levels of service will be developed that will be independent of technology, but will be based instead on staff time required.

This is a tough, and possibly controversial, prediction. It suggests a redefinition of what we do as librarians.

Basically public libraries now perform two types of service. The first might be termed *passive*. By that I mean we provide the materials, the indexes, the finding mechanisms, and control tools that make it possible for individuals to find a book or research an issue. The professional skills needed to support this type of service are largely behind the scenes (book selection, cataloging, acquisitions, etc.), and because these activities are invisible our users often make the mistake of assuming that all librarians do is "stamp out books." This false assumption has led to an undervaluing of library work and the attendant difficulty we have securing adequate pay.

The second type of service we provide might be called *active*. Here we provide answers to questions, not just access to materials containing those answers. Most libraries provide reference services both by phone and on a walk-in basis. Usually the service is a kind of ready reference with either explicit or implied limits placed on the amount of time to be spent with any one patron. The response of our users to this sort of service is in marked contrast to the usual response to our passive services. Typically a patron is impressed with the skill of the librarian and often grateful for the service.

Many public libraries are now offering the beginnings of a third type of service that I would like to call *interactive*. In present library configurations this generally consists of a database search. The service is usually not well publicized and the user is charged by connect time and other computer-related expenses. This service is highly professional and intensely interactive. It requires more time than we generally allot to ready reference. Because of the staff time required, most libraries provide this service rather reluctantly. Some even go so far as to make it available only once a week or at some other specified period of time that negates the advantage a computer offers in providing quick information. Most of our patrons are unaware that public libraries provide this service.

The present policy of charging for computer searches is a bad idea. It is a policy we cannot and should not continue for two very different reasons: (1) As standard reference materials become available exclusively in machine-readable form, fees will be imposed for information that was previously available for free. This places the library in a position of providing information only to those who can pay and overlooks some significant cost

savings libraries may realize by moving from print to electronic storage and access. (2) While we are charging for machine access we are unwilling to assess a fee based on level of service. This policy is preventing us from providing interactive services in any meaningful way and is limiting our ability to make the best use of available technology. It is easy to charge for connect time but the practice is distorting the service we provide, depriving our communities of important benefits, and, if continued, will push the library further and further to the periphery of society.

The public library of the future will continue to provide passive, active, and interactive services. The definition of these services will not, however, be based on the extent of computer use, but will depend instead on the amount and level of professional assistance required.

Forecast 6

Fee-based, interactive research services will be developed.

Is there anyone who still doubts that the challenge of the day is not to get information, but to get the right information? As the sheer volume of information threatens to overtake our ability to manage it in any form, the specific piece of needed information has become increasingly elusive.

I am reminded of an incident that dramatically illustrates the point. During the course of planning for the White House Conference on Library and Information Services (1979), we decided to send delegates information about all the legislation currently before the U.S. Congress concerning libraries and information services. After an extensive search, a conference staffer appeared in my office carrying a three-foot stack of paper, dropped it in the middle of the floor, and said "Here it is, what do you want me to do with it?" After additional inspection we discovered that what we wanted was not the three-foot stack, but the information contained in approximately one inch of the stack.

No institution provides people as skilled in the extraction of that one inch of information as the library. Librarians are trained to do reference, and yet we put them in libraries and tell them to spend no more than a few minutes on each inquiry.

Meanwhile businesses are clamoring for help. A fee-based research service is a logical step. Although such a service will probably be heavily dependent on computer databases and related technologies, the fee will be based as much on time expended as it would on pass-through computer-related costs.

Librarians frequently undervalue their own time. In Atlanta, as in other cities, we make a practice of responding fully to queries from elected officials. Recently a librarian spent two days looking for information concerning a zoning question for one of our county commissioners. After failing to find the information requested in printed form she searched one of the databases available to us and found the answer in thirty minutes. Surely two days of her time is worth far more than the charge for a thirty-minute search.

Nevertheless most public librarians do not feel that they are authorized to start with the computer search. That we permit this situation to continue is an institutional failing that is making us less effective than we can be in meeting the needs of our users.

A fee-based service that charges for human search time will help remedy this situation. It will become obvious that a database search is very often a faster and less costly way to get needed information. Businesses are already aware of this and have asked us to institute a fee-based service as soon as possible. They tell us that the most expensive solution to their information problems is to send one of their employees to the library to do research. They would much prefer to pay the library with its experienced searchers to get the answers to their questions.

Objections to the institution of a fee-based service usually come from two quarters: those who claim that such a service would discriminate against those who cannot pay, and those who claim that such a service would unfairly compete with private information providers.

These are important issues that are well worth our collective, professional attention. Free access to information is a cornerstone of the library ethic. This author is not suggesting that fees be levied for services now being provided without charge. The issue is who pays, and for what.

Collectively, through tax revenue, we pay for the services described above as passive and active. Most libraries are not providing interactive services in any meaningful way at all. Thus fees will be charged for new services that the library is unable to provide for free. There would be no reduction in current, free services. Moreover, with the redefinition of services outlined above, there would be no charge for simple computer searches for which many libraries currently levy a charge. Access to materials in either print or electronic form would be unrestricted. Fees would be assessed at a "level of effort" required by library staff.

From a management point of view, this service should be established as a separate, self-supporting unit within the library. This structural element would help eliminate service ambiguity and ensure cost accountability. A business or an individual would deal directly with the search service staff to clearly outline the information needed and set limits on the amount of money that could be spent.

The charge that such a service would compete unfairly with private information providers ignores two facts. Private information providers are not now meeting the needs of the community, and private information providers rely heavily on publicly supported libraries to fill the needs of their own clients. The service seems to me to be a clear extension of the role of the library and is justifiable on that basis.

In addition to the obvious value to those who will use the service, a sophisticated fee-based service offers other benefits. It brings the library into the economic mainstream of the community, broadens the revenue base available, and makes the value of library work more obvious. Far from eroding the base of public support, I forecast that the institution of this service will contribute to the public awareness that promotes public support.

Forecast 7

A new job title of "Information Specialist" will be introduced into the public library.

For years librarians have struggled with the need to provide alternative career paths for expert librarians who are not interested in becoming administrators. The development of an information specialist job title will provide such a career path, help in the continuing struggle for adequate salaries, and give us an opportunity to compete with the private sector for some of the top graduates of our library schools.

The librarian series of jobs will be filled by generalists, branch librarians, and administrators. The information specialist series will be filled by librarians having significant background and experience in information technology and special subject areas.

Forecast 8

Book circulation will continue to be an important part of library services.

For all the talk about technology, books will continue to be the backbone of the library. As electronic storage and transmission of data grows, the need for books will expand, not contract. The layering of technology is a common phenomenon. Historically, developments in communications technology have not replaced older forms but have existed and continue to exist in a symbiotic relationship with each complementing the other. Thus we find in our current environment that radio, television, film, video, telephone, mail, and books all continue to fill specific roles in our lives.

Forecast 9

Public libraries will not only survive, they will flourish.

People love libraries. No institution in the community serves so many in such a positive way. Nevertheless, the last decade has been a struggle for many libraries that have faced massive budget cuts and the resulting deterioration of services. Out of this bleak period, however, we have learned something about political power and have gained some skill in using it. Perhaps most important, we have learned that we have a professional and ethical obligation to ask for the resources we need to provide adequate library service to the community we serve.

Libraries have advantages available to few other public institutions. We are in every neighborhood, we are a continuing positive force, and we serve people of every age (no small factor as America grays). The library of the future will be increasingly sensitive to the public it serves. It will ask for the support it needs to provide services. It will use the natural political power base that flows from its position in the community to fulfill its public obligations.

The public library of the future will build on the best of the past and take advantage of the political and technological opportunities of the present to create a future in which libraries provide the information and knowledge that encourages people to search for wisdom.

3

The Future Revisited

A reporter asked why Cleveland was spending $90 million on a new main library complex when everyone would soon get all their information electronically. I replied with two words: equity and access. Although electronic technologies are dramatically changing the way libraries do business, not everyone has a computer and much information has not yet been digitized. The interaction took me back to nine predictions I made in *LJ* some eleven years ago ("The Future of the Public Library," *LJ*, September 1, 1985, p. 136–39). They were based on expected technological change within the context of economic constraints and political realities.

The 1985 Predictions

1. The public library of the future will be judged not by the size of its collection, but by its success in providing information quickly and accurately.

Here I forecasted the current shift from ownership to access, and the debate that followed. Libraries now clearly emphasize access far more than they did in 1985, but we are also beginning to appreciate some of the limitations of digitized information even as we climb aboard the World Wide Web (WWW) bandwagon. A decade ago and be-

Reprinted from *Library Journal*, July 1996. Copyright © 1996, Reed Elsevier Inc.

fore, access usually meant interlibrary loan, with its cumbersome processes and long delays. Now when we talk about access we think immediately of electronic access.

One of the developments that has helped public libraries move more effectively into the provision of electronic access has been the inauguration of subscription-based pricing for some electronic databases. Libraries are understandably reluctant to subscribe to services that charge on a per search basis because they have no way to budget for such an open-ended item.

Success in some areas does not necessarily mean we will ultimately have electronic access to all human knowledge. There are limitations on what can and should be digitized. One limitation is size and scope. To cite one example: the Library of Congress (LC) has embarked on a program to digitize some portions of its 100 million-item collection at the rate of roughly a million items a year. At that rate, if LC adds nothing, it would take one hundred years to convert the collection. One might argue that working together using the model of the OCLC bibliographic database, libraries could digitize the world's literature more quickly.

2. Within ten years, over half of the services provided to library users will be to individuals who never come into the library.

Although the forecast accurately saw the direction of future library service, it was wrong about the rate of change. Libraries have not yet developed electronic service in the depth and breadth anticipated. At the Cleveland Public Library (CPL), remote searches currently account for about seventy thousand (7 percent) of the one million searches per month on our system.

The real surprise is not the low percentage of external use but the relationship between the growth of the library's electronic library and that of conventional use of the library. Apparently, the more we provide electronically the more people use the library conventionally. Walk-in use of the library is up, circulation is up, and the growth curves parallel each other, suggesting a causal relationship between them and electronic services. This reinforces the idea that print and electronic information fill different needs.

3. Public libraries will develop an information infrastructure to provide access to a growing and changing flow of information.

Libraries and their suppliers had already begun to build regional and local networks and systems in 1985, and that work continued. However, technological progress leapfrogged these efforts, and the Internet and the WWW provide new options. Libraries were thus liberated from total dependence on library networks. They now take advantage of many network options, a host of new devices, and software to exploit electronic information resources worldwide.

4. This infrastructure will include more, smaller library branches.

Although more, smaller branches would seem to be a natural outgrowth of our ability to make smaller facilities more functional using computer and communications technologies, in fact, the number of library branches in most systems has not changed. The forecast neglected to note that whether or not a pattern of smaller units is adopted is still a political rather than a technological decision.

In an urban setting it is still true that resources are better spent on smaller branches that are closer to the people they serve. Even in rural areas, smaller, free-standing libraries now have the capability to offer a far greater range of services.

5. Levels of service will be developed that will be independent of technology but will be based instead on staff time required.

6. Fee-based, interactive research services will be developed.

When these predictions were made it was common for libraries to charge for computer searches because they were costly and many still regarded them as an ancillary service. The forecasts predicted a time when computer searches would be as normal as looking for the answer to a reference question in a book. That time has surely arrived. More and more libraries provide free Internet access to their users. Today a great deal of information is only available electronically, and charging for electronic access would be as antithetical to the library's mission as charging to read a newspaper or check out a book. The issue is—and has always been—equity.

The forecasts did come true to some extent as some libraries do charge for subsets of services based on staff time involved rather than computer connect time. While there is still debate about whether a public library should charge for any reference service, those that do charge tend to base their fees on the time it takes to provide the service, with some additional cost recovery for computer connect time when there is a discrete charge for it.

At CPL our decision to provide a fee-based service was predicated on our goal to be the first place anyone thinks to go for any information at all. Rather than turn people away who want time-consuming and specialized research, we choose to provide the service for a fee. Businesses are the most frequent users of the service, mostly because they would rather pay us than do the research themselves.

7. A new job title of "information specialist" will be introduced into the public library.

This was a silly attempt to capture the notion that librarians did more than handle books. It is sillier now. Today librarians find answers to questions in whatever format they exist, and there is a noticeable return to the earlier image of a librarian as a wise person, a navigator, a guide through the maze of ignorance. Today the role of that kind of a librarian, with its history and substance, is much more appealing than that of an information techie.

8. Book circulation will continue to be an important part of library services.

Yes, but. . . . There is no question that books and electronic resources will work together in libraries to communicate knowledge, not just information. The use of book-lending counts—circulation statistics as the measure of library activity—will and should be abandoned.

9. Public libraries will not only survive, they will flourish.

In the past ten years, public libraries have been through some bad times but have not just survived, they have flourished. Even as the pundits of the virtual future predict the disappearance of libraries in the vapors of cyberspace, citizens all across the country are rebuilding their libraries. Los Angeles, Denver, San Francisco, Chicago, Phoenix, San Antonio, and Cleveland, to mention only a few, have built big, new, contemporary main library buildings. It is a tribute to the public's view of what is the best investment of public dollars. Great new libraries are symbols of the importance of knowledge and learning. Can all these citizens be wrong? Certainly not.

The Decade Ahead

If technology has been the driving force for change over the last decade, the driving force for the coming decade is more technology. The mission of the library—to provide access to information for everyone in the community when and where the individual needs it—remains intact. While different libraries articulate their missions to emphasize different aspects of their service, they continue to be more alike than different. That is good. People across the country recognize a common library mission, and they celebrate it time after time, in place after place, when they vote to build and support more, better public libraries.

Although the library mission stays the same, the way we achieve it has changed dramatically, and will change even more dramatically in the decade ahead. To see the future, put that traditional public library mission into a modern, electronic world. Then the issues of the future emerge.

Collection Building and Organization

The emphasis on access over ownership will continue. While electronic access is unlikely to replace the book collection in the near future (or ever), some categories of information and knowledge will become totally digital. Data (statistics, lists, stock market quotations, anything that is immediate, changing, hard to keep up with in print, and distinct—requiring no abstract or conceptual thought) will go electronic. Digital sources will be used for information specific to one person or institution (home pages that provide more localized information than would be economical to print and distribute widely). Primary source material unavailable to casual researchers or students because of the fragile nature of the material or the remoteness of the holdings will be available in electronic formats. Articles now published in scholarly journals will be disseminated online. Electronic access to these materials, supplemented by network access to the print holdings of libraries anywhere, will bring new information riches within the grasp of every elementary, high school, and college student and their parents and teachers.

In the next decade the current chaos of the Internet and WWW will become better organized. The job may be accomplished by library consortia or by commercial vendors. Without better organization, the vast information highway will become one long, boring traffic jam.

Librarians have long excelled at organizing knowledge. Many argue that the Internet and the Web are a new paradigm and that organization will slowly emerge out of chaos; that systematic classification of knowledge is outmoded, and Boolean search capabilities, hypertext, expert systems, and their cousins will revolutionize the way we think about the organization of knowledge. That may be true, but so far it seems that the more there is on the Web, the harder it is to find. Lately, even simple searches yield many hundreds of hits, most of which have nothing to do with the subject being searched. New search engines are beginning to look more and more like old classification schemes in electronic clothing. While the graphics are from *Star Wars*, the content is from LC.

Preservation and Access

In the next few years a centralized service will be developed to warehouse backup tapes, preservation microfilm, or even paper, as a kind of insurance policy against the possibility of digital deletion.

Electronic preservation is an increasingly troubling issue for the whole profession. Electronic journals (journals initially published in electronic format) are not necessarily retained by their publishers. The paper originals of materials published initially in print and later digitized are often discarded, since one reason to digitize is to save space. Yet preservation librarians worry about the long-term stability of the electronic medium. No one really knows how long it will last, or if it makes sense to institute conversions as soon as each new format becomes obsolete.

There is widespread concern about the loss of a paper trail as e-mail replaces paper and vanishes at the touch of a "delete" key. You don't have to be a Luddite to fear that we are in danger of losing our history.

The reemergence of reading rooms, especially in public libraries, will be the result of library efforts to fulfill the long-standing mission to provide equity of access to information for all citizens. This was a fundamental purpose for the founding of U.S. public libraries. Public libraries and democratic governments have always walked hand in hand, and equity of access is their most important concern.

One can envision, indeed one can already see in some places, banks of PCs where study tables once stood. Students and adults of all ages increasingly spend time in the library reading the information provided via the Internet.

Because so much is available only electronically, libraries must provide the electronic connection just as they once provided books for those who could not afford to buy them. The current situation is analogous to the one we had at the beginning of this century, when people came in to libraries to read—not just to borrow material but actually to read the material.

Libraries as Publishers

Libraries are likely to become electronic publishers of information, as they work with local government and other organizations to digitize public documents. In CPL, we have already posted candidate information provided by the League of Women Voters and are working with a local hospital watchdog group to mount information about the performance of local hospitals. We are also exploring the possibility of listing city information about real estate transactions and are beginning to digitize local history documents.

Copyright

Reasoned negotiations will ultimately replace the hostile posturing that marks the differences between copyright "owners" and the library, research, and education communities. The greatest impediment to realizing the promise of digitization and electronic transmission is copyright. Article I of the Constitution states that the Congress can secure "for limited times to authors and inventors the exclusive right to their respective writings and discoveries . . ." in order "to promote the progress of science and useful arts. . . ."

Few would argue with the wisdom of that enactment, but when electronic technologies are used to store and transmit documents, definitions become blurred. The Association of American Publishers has argued that any electronic transmission of a document is a copy, protected by copyright law, and subject to copyright payment. Various library groups have argued that the fair use doctrine, which permits limited copying under carefully constrained circumstances, enables less restricted copying for education and scholarship. Both sides claim they are pursuing the constitutional mandate to "promote the progress of science and the useful arts." To date, both sides of the copyright debate have maintained and even toughened their positions. The litigation that has occurred so far has not provided a definitive way out of the copyright war. Ultimately, the various stakeholders will have to reason together, since neither can afford to fight out the remaining differences in court.

Training and Measurement

Libraries will spend increasing amounts on training. In fact, any library that spends significant amounts on hardware, software, and communications lines without investing in staff training is throwing money away. As the rate of change in technology continues unabated, we find that we must replace equipment every two to three years. In Cleveland that means we must retrain staff every year. If staff are uncomfortable with new technology, they will feel threatened. If staff are comfortable with new tools, they will feel empow-

ered by them, and they will be able to help the public use them effectively.

Library staff will find new ways to measure and report the massive change in the way people now use libraries. Because the public is accustomed to thinking about circulation, we will be best served by incorporating electronic circulation into traditional circulation figures.

When a student does research today, he or she searches magazines online and prints out copies of the articles wanted. The student may go on to search other databases and print out the findings. The student gets much more information than with traditional print sources, but the library credits itself with no circulation at all. The library has done a better job meeting the student's needs than it did five years ago, but when it is compared statistically with other libraries, it looks as if it is falling behind.

We'd Invent Them

The Council on Library Resources (CLR) received 292 responses to a recent request for information on the use of electronic technologies in public libraries. They came from libraries of all sizes nationwide and told of low-cost projects and regional transformations of library service. Case studies on twelve sites are being drafted by CLR staff for publication to the profession. As chair of the committee overseeing this effort, I was impressed by the range and extent of activity in large and small, rural and urban, rich and poor libraries—in libraries of every location and description imaginable. Libraries are not only willing to change, they are on the cutting edge in applying technology.

Public librarians have discovered, no, created and built both the infrastructure and the local systems to bring information and knowledge in print and on the screen to the people in their communities. So crucial is this role that if public libraries did not already exist, we would have to invent them.

PART II

Political Context

Politics is not just a problem for public libraries, as anyone from academia will be happy to tell you. Politics is about more than government and who gets elected; it is about relationships of a very special sort. Politics is about relationships of power. It is about control. It is about winning and losing and forging relationships that will lead to success in a power-driven society. The political context in which libraries operate gives us our governance structures, our funding, our support for moving libraries forward. Politics creates the public perception of what libraries are and how well they do.

The first three chapters in this section promote very specific programs as avenues for libraries to use in seeking appropriate power. The first explores the benefits of aligning libraries with Regional Councils of Government, while the second discusses the benefits of a White House Conference. While some might dispute the benefits of both, the articles contain an embedded conviction that libraries ought to establish productive relationships with local and national elected officials. The first chapter asserts that "to function effectively, it is necessary to consider the nature of power, the source of power, and the most effective means of acquiring it." Even today the notion that libraries ought to aggressively acquire power has a slightly subversive sound to it. The second chapter claims that we ought to go beyond establishing relationships with elected officials to involving citizens themselves in library business. While even I might now argue with the relative effectiveness of the means espoused in these two chapters, the goals seem to me to remain valid today, and I have included them more for the questions they raise than the answers they suggest. I have included the third article, "The Fortune Cookie," because it reminds us of the "state of creative tension" that exists between the public and private sectors, and for the reminder borrowed from Douglas Hofstadter that the "fortune lies as much in the hand of the eater as in the cookie."

In 1981 I wrote a series of columns for *Library Journal* called "Washington Update," in which I explored a number of topics that I found provocative at the time. In rereading these, I found some dated while others contain material that remains relevant today. I have included my four favorites in this book. The first, "A View from the Right," is here not for its description of the Reagan legislative initiative but for its enunciation of those "inexorable laws that dictate and mediate political change." It seems to me that the laws of bureaucratic inertia, maximum convergence, and political expediency are still governing the never-ending dance of legislation in Washington, state capitals, cities, and universities around the globe. "The Prisoner's Dilemma" applies a classic model used in game theory to library strategy. As it makes explicit what many of us experience implicitly, I thought it might make for a spirited discussion. "Information and Public Policy" describes one attempt to elevate and establish information policy as part of our ongoing national dialogue. The bill described failed (largely because of the laws outlined in the first column), but the need remains. Information policy continues to inform many of our laws and, today, even our treaties. Finally, "Research: The Lumber Yard Approach" describes one attempt to develop a research agenda for libraries. This was not the first and will certainly not be the last time library professionals have undertaken this daunting task. To my knowledge these efforts have never been successful, no matter how well intentioned the sponsor or how talented the participants. This suggests that the process itself is flawed, and the article may still have the power to provoke discussion.

The final article in this section, "Politics and the Public Library," was written as a practical guide for public library directors and those aspiring to be a public library director. Subsequent to its publication, however, I found that librarians in academic and private sector environments also found ideas, suggestions, and observations that proved useful. In many ways this essay demonstrates the importance of trend analysis in guiding an institution through the challenges that each day brings.

Any discussion of political context must, by definition, generate a variety of perspectives. Questions abound, from the theoretical to the practical. These might include:

- What is power?
- Should libraries seek power? Why? Why not?
- Should some power relationships be avoided? Give some examples.
- Today, how can libraries align themselves with those exercising power?
- Do the laws of legislation still apply?
- How can the prisoner's dilemma help improve understanding of a difficult situation?
- Do we need a national information policy?
- Is a national research agenda a good idea? Why? Why not? What are some alternatives?

Whether we enjoy politics or not, it conditions our environment. An understanding of power relationships is useful, and sometimes critical, in moving an institution forward. That does not mean it is always comfortable. Still, it is better to know than not know, better to be informed than be naive, better to be aware than be surprised. Politics isn't the only thing, but it is one of the most important things.

4

The Politics of Cooperation

Politics, to paraphrase Gibbon, is easier to deplore than to describe. Indeed, in recent months, even the concept of cooperation has become suspect.

In spite of the fact that library cooperatives are fast developing throughout the country, and many librarians feel that the potential for cooperation has yet to be fully exploited, there is an equally strong, alarmingly intense feeling for localism. Ken Beasley, graduate school dean at the University of Texas at El Paso, enunciated this position at the American Library Association Convention in Las Vegas when he declared that cooperation has gone as far as it can. This, of course, is the kind of statement that is sure to raise the ire of any self-respecting, liberal thinking, cooperative minded librarian. And yet it is also the kind of statement which should not be dismissed out of hand.

Perhaps cooperation, or at least the kind of cooperation libraries have traditionally participated in, has gone as far as it can go. The essential consideration is the nature of the cooperative endeavor.

Generally, libraries participate in loose federations of libraries. In addition to providing a forum for the exchange of information and an approach to coordinated library planning,

library cooperatives generally develop special projects which are designed to satisfy three basic objectives: (1) increase available resources, (2) extend the accessibility of those resources, and (3) diminish costs.

Within this context libraries agree to more efficient interlibrary loan procedures, universal library cards, metropolitan delivery systems, cooperative acquisition agreements, and in some sophisticated systems the centralization of selected services. As valuable as these things are to the development of library service, they represent an approach to only one aspect of the problem, the relationship of one library to another library, and are therefore self-limiting.

Another aspect, and one which may well prove crucial to libraries, has to do with the relationship of libraries in general to the total social picture and especially to other public agencies. It is in this area that most library cooperatives as they are presently established are ineffective.

In his recent *LJ* article, Louis Vagianos suggested that one of the two overriding problems in the profession today has to do with "the problems related to the lack of political control librarians have over their own destinies." We are indeed attempting to function within a "philosophy of powerlessness" at a time when we should be seeking new avenues to power. But to function effectively it

Reprinted from *Library Journal*, November 1, 1973.
Copyright © 1973, Reed Elsevier Inc.

is necessary to consider the nature of power, the source of power, and the most effective means of acquiring it.

The libraries and library cooperatives to which I am referring here are those that exist in the huge metropolitan areas of the country. While this concern undoubtedly expresses a personal bias, this bias is not entirely without foundation. Metropolitan areas have in fact become the great centers of our population.

In 1900 there were approximately 75 million Americans, and only 40 percent lived in urban areas. Today the population of the United States is almost 200 million, and the percentage living in urban environments is in excess of 70 percent. It is predicted that, by the year 2000, 85 percent of the population of this country will reside in urban metropolitan areas.

Retreat to the Suburbs

Within these metropolitan areas certain tensions (economic and social) have developed. The flight of the white middle class as well as industry out of the central city coupled with the revenue problems of almost every core city have highlighted the difficulty.

These broad governmental concerns are directly related to the problems of libraries in metropolitan areas. A large, old, under-supported central city library system surrounded by shining new, well-supported suburban libraries has become a cliché.

The total situation is further aggravated by the recent emphasis on localism. We have witnessed Supreme Court decisions that prescribe local definitions of morality, federal funding patterns that emphasize local autonomy, and a seemingly pervasive feeling that one may retreat from the overwhelming problems of a city or a region into the relative security of a well-feathered nest in the suburbs.

These retreats, however, are unrealistic. Problems of air pollution don't stop at city lines; transportation inadequacies impinge on suburban comfort; and even libraries are discovering an interdependence between those in the city and those in the adjoining jurisdictions.

In a recent interview with the *Washington Post,* Norman Finkler, director of the Montgomery County, Maryland, Public Library noted, "We are living off the big cities. We are less likely to buy specialized materials because we know we can borrow from Washington and Baltimore when they are needed. So we concentrate on other items."

It is this concentration on other items which has helped boost the circulation for Montgomery County to 9.7 books per capita—the highest in the nation.

Interdependence is further demonstrated by the Fairfax County, Virginia, Public Library (another Washington suburb) where a system of sixteen branches has been developed with no central library. The necessary duplication of titles has resulted in system holdings of 822,665 volumes with only 138,334 unique titles. On the other hand, the Martin Luther King, Jr., Memorial Library in the District of Columbia has 545,393 volumes, with approximately 300,000 different titles.

Clearly libraries in a region do depend on each other, with the inner-city system frequently providing backup support from ever diminishing resources.

The problems of libraries in metropolitan regions are different from those of libraries in more rural parts of the country in degree if not in kind, and demand different solutions.

Norton Lang has written: "The future of the Metropolis is the future of most of us. The quality of life that is lived in it is the quality of American life. . . . The question at issue is whether we have the wit, the courage, the good sense, and the good will to transform the 200-odd Metropolitan areas in which the bulk of us live into responsibly self-governing communities."

The Regional Council

One approach which has been developed to deal with the areawide problems which beset metropolitan regions is Regional Councils of Government—voluntary organizations of municipalities and counties. Between 1968 and 1969 the National Service to Regional

Councils reported that COGs (defined as councils of governing bodies containing a majority of locally elected officials) grew from 100 to 175 in number. By 1971 there were over 300. Almost every one of the nation's 247 Standard Metropolitan Statistical Areas (SMSAs) has a Regional Council of some type (COGs, Economic Development Districts, Regional Planning Commissions, etc.).

A Regional Council is not another level of government, but instead provides a mechanism whereby local elected officials may discuss common problems and regional issues. These councils grew out of the recognized need to develop a regionwide consensus and to promote coordinated cooperative action among the independent jurisdictions regarding those problems which cannot be solved by any single government.

Regional Councils are supported by local jurisdictions and grants from federal and state agencies. In addition, these organizations have been strengthened by federal legislation which supports the planning and reviewing functions of the councils. Nevertheless, they still have no real power to implement programs, but depend for their success on cooperation and persuasion.

Regional Councils have been particularly active in the areas of housing, transportation, and regional planning. More and more, however, they are involving themselves with the total environment of an area.

Library Regionalism

If we really believe that information is an important part of the regional environment, we must be willing to act as if we believe it. Comprehensive regional library service must be approached in its entirety and in context—as a technical, administrative, and political system that interacts with the larger community of which it is a part.

It is time for libraries to see themselves in this role, to think about cooperating with nonlibrary officials, and to affiliate themselves with these Regional Councils. While other forms of library cooperation have been extensive and at times effective, it is this political element which has been overlooked. It is, I think, significant that of the over three hundred Regional Councils in the country only three (Denver, Baltimore, and Washington) have any involvement with libraries.

While regional agencies vary considerably in their organization and effectiveness, they generally include certain technical committees to advise the elected officials in specific matters. It is, therefore, the task of a Librarians' Technical Committee to advise and support the council with respect to the informational needs of a region.

Library committees affiliated in this manner operate in much the same fashion as independent library cooperatives. Projects may be devised and implemented, information may be exchanged, and common problems discussed, all independent from the total council.

It is only when this committee wishes the endorsement of its Regional Council that the total organization is involved. And it is at this point that political considerations come into play.

In addition to cooperative programs involving only libraries, there are other activities in which libraries may participate which are specific to regional planning agencies. The most obvious is the inclusion of libraries in the whole regional planning process.

Since it is the business of a Regional Council to plan for regional growth and development and produce reports to that effect, it seems appropriate that the chief information resource, the library, be included. It is, in fact, an exceedingly frustrating experience to read report after regional report that fails to acknowledge the existence of libraries or the need of people in the region for information.

Council Resources

From a pragmatic point of view, a COG has a variety of technical expertise available which may be exploited by library cooperatives affiliated with the agency. Information data banks are frequently available and can be extraordinarily helpful. Public relations people and graphic artists can assist in the development and distribution of appropriate publicity. There are even people available who can assist in the development and selling of proposals.

Staff interaction in a more general sense is also an important asset to the library cooperative. Support staff for the library committee may interact with other planning staff in a whole variety of ways, both by influencing and by being influenced. Regional planners begin to think of libraries and information needs of the community in connection with housing, transportation, and even planned open spaces. At the same time the library planner or projects coordinator necessarily begins to think of total developmental plans and criteria when dealing with library projects or problems.

As Jean Anne South, library planner for the Baltimore Regional Planning Council, put it, ". . . when you sit at a meeting where sewers, transportation, and health problems are discussed as well as libraries, you begin to see correlations."

It becomes evident after a while that public agencies of all types are faced with problems in which there are more similarities than differences. Like public health services, recreation departments and other municipal services, libraries are faced with a fragmented pattern of support involving state, local, and sometimes federal monies. Goals are diffuse and sometimes conflicting. Power rests in the hands of the politicians.

Politics and Politicians

A final consideration, and perhaps the most significant one, has to do with political access. As has been pointed out earlier, Councils of Government have everything to do with local politicians. The various policy-making committees as well as the Board of Directors are composed of local elected officials.

Since an important goal of librarians must be to achieve greater public support, access to those individuals who determine and interpret public policy is very valuable indeed. Monthly progress reports relating the activities of the library committee generate interest in libraries in a nondemanding and nonthreatening environment. In view of the fact that libraries are not autonomous but do depend for their very existence on the informed goodwill of the elected officials, the importance of this function should not be underestimated. There are, of course, disadvantages as well to this approach to library cooperation. The most obvious problem is the bureaucratic structure of the agency.

In seeking funding for a cooperative library project, for instance, it is necessary not only to obtain a consensus from the libraries involved, but agency approval must be obtained as well. The process can sometimes take several months, involves several policy committees composed of numerous politicians, and can be an exhausting experience.

In spite of the frustrations involved, however, there are some very positive aspects to this procedure. Whether funding is ultimately achieved or not, libraries and information services are brought to the attention of a number of people. Problems and possible solutions are acknowledged. Ongoing programs in local jurisdictions are recognized. Sometimes very helpful suggestions are made with respect to funding sources with which some individual has connections.

Because Regional Councils have no power apart from the power to persuade, the persuasive ability is highly developed. The techniques employed, while not very different than those used by sociologists and anthropologists, are fascinating to observe in an urban political setting.

No matter what techniques are employed, however, there are abiding tensions that exist among adjoining jurisdictions, and cooperation is not always easy. Vested interests and competing goals make common solutions difficult and sometimes impossible. Frequently difficulties are encountered when a jurisdiction is required to contribute money or to relinquish autonomy in some area. The recognition of a problem does not insure a solution.

In Washington, the Council of Governments is responsible for monitoring the pollution level in the region and announcing air pollution alerts when appropriate. Nevertheless COG has no power to take actions which would diminish the danger, but can only suggest that area residents take voluntary action which will contribute to the possibility of continued breathing.

The Librarians' Technical Committee has been trying for some years to achieve a universal library card for the region. While the concept has indeed received wide support and the majority of libraries in the area do participate, there are still a few jurisdictions whose libraries do not. The District of Columbia Public Library is prohibited by Congress from cooperating; and other libraries have local political reasons for nonparticipation.

Some years ago the library profession recognized interdependence of libraries of all types and developed what John Cory has christened a third generation of library organization. But there is also an interdependence between libraries and other public agencies. This recognition forms the basis for a fourth generation of library organization. Affiliation with a Regional Council is undoubtedly not the only road we may take, but it is one way we should explore.

Approaches to Affiliation

The affiliation of a library cooperative with a Regional Council is not a complex or legalistic maneuver. In Washington the marriage came about almost casually when Henry Drennan, a cooperative-minded librarian with the Division of Library Services of the United States Office of Education, and Mary Marshall, a local politician and member of the Council of Governments, began discussing regional library problems. A meeting with the Executive Director of the Council of Governments was arranged and the Librarians' Technical Committee soon developed.

In most instances an informal meeting between the Executive Director of the Regional Council and a representative of the library group interested in affiliating is all that is necessary. Information may be exchanged and the possibility of cooperation examined. Since patterns of cooperation depend heavily on the geographic and demographic characteristics of a region and the organization of the Regional Council involved, mechanisms of affiliation will vary.

In the development of these regional cooperatives no rigid pattern is apparent, nor is one likely to develop, given the variety of needs and circumstances present in different parts of the country.

The Denver Librarians Committee has approached the matter of cooperation in a very different fashion from Baltimore or Washington and has in fact developed a regional system. This approach has worked well for Denver and has resulted in programs such as the municipal government reference center, a program for continuing education, and extensive interlibrary loan and reciprocal borrowing arrangements. A union catalog and periodical list are now in planning stages. The overriding advantage to the affiliation, according to Edward Sayre, the system director, is the interaction with planners and municipal government specialists.

The approach in Baltimore has been somewhat less structured. Since the state of Maryland has a quite well developed state library plan, with Enoch Pratt in Baltimore designated as a state resource, the problems and challenges are slightly different. The result has been a series of studies. The latest, *Information Needs of Urban Residents,* funded by the United States Office of Education and scheduled to be released in the next few months, promises to be a significant contribution to the whole question of information services in urban areas.

As the center of the federal government, Washington is always in a unique position. The metropolitan area is composed of fifteen jurisdictions in three states. Since anything involving the District itself requires approval of

Congress as well, any kind of cooperation is a challenge. Nevertheless members of the Librarians' Technical Committee have shown themselves to be consummate politicians on more than one occasion and have developed a *Research Design for Library Cooperative Planning and Action in the Metropolitan Area,* portions of which are presently being implemented.

In addition, the group has achieved reciprocal borrowing agreements, daily delivery of library materials, and a joint purchasing agreement which has saved several thousands of dollars on the purchase of mylar book jackets. Most recently the three states signed a contract with COG for staff support of the Librarians' Technical Committee.

From the beginning Drennan saw the goals of the committee as: (1) to involve all types of libraries in the development of mechanisms for cooperation; (2) to institute certain research and demonstration projects; and most important (3) to increase political access for librarians. It was his feeling that librarians should be recognized as department heads with substantial claims upon the attention of the politicians. They need, according to Drennan, "a more visible place in the political process."

Politics in this country is the process whereby power is exercised, and libraries must recognize power as a desirable and necessary goal. Political interaction, however, is difficult to evaluate. Library directors already deal with their local elected officials on a regular basis for the purpose of obtaining appropriations. The inclusion of libraries in a total regional planning approach and the interaction with politicians and other public agencies which this implies offer another level of political activity. The importance of this level of activity is something which each region must decide for itself. It may be that the full impact will not be felt for some time.

But now is the time for us to think about the direction in which we would like to see libraries move. With the expiration of the Library Services and Construction Act in 1976 we might like to push for legislation which would encourage and support regional development, looking to the eventuality of a national library network.

We might also like to examine the form which regional library cooperation should take. COGs are growing, in number and effectiveness. They bring together the representatives of local political power and employ highly sophisticated forms of persuasion to bring about common solutions to regional problems. Libraries should be a part of this process.

5

The Politics of Information

A popular government, without popular information or the means of acquiring it, is but a prologue to a farce or a tragedy or perhaps both. Knowledge will forever govern ignorance, and a people who mean to be their own governors must arm themselves with the power which knowledge gives.

—James Madison, Fourth President of the United States

We, like Madison, live in a dangerous age. However, the dimensions of the danger have changed. On November 15 of this year, close to two thousand delegates, alternates, and observers will assemble in Washington to participate in the first White House Conference on Library and Information Services. In the course of their deliberations they will address some of the most pressing issues facing our country today—information issues. The significance of the conference, however, goes far beyond the issues to be addressed. To fully grasp the importance of this conference we must understand that it is part of a political process. Viewed from a narrow perspective, that process began in 1957 when Channing Bete suggested that such a conference should be held. It proceeded through fifty-seven pre-White House Conferences, will culminate in Washington in November, and will continue when the conference is over. From a broader perspective, political action is fundamental to decision making in this country. This article will discuss why this conference is especially

Reprinted from *Library Journal*, September 15, 1979. Copyright © 1979, Reed Elsevier Inc.

significant, what we hope to achieve, and how change can be accomplished.

To fully appreciate the importance of the White House Conference we must understand the role of libraries in our society, the importance of information to every individual, and recent technological changes which affect the collection and distribution of that information.

Information Justice

The role of libraries in this country has always been to serve as custodians of social value and to act as agencies of information justice. Libraries are in fact the only institutions in our country that offer a wide spectrum of information to the individual seeking it rather than a narrow band of information to a wide audience. Librarians feel deeply that their mission is to provide information to anyone who walks through the door. If our form of government requires an informed public, the mission of libraries is to provide the source of that information, equally to all.

This role has not changed. We still must maintain a collective history and social value, and the need for information justice has never been more evident. But the environment in which libraries must operate has changed drastically and will most certainly affect the ways in which libraries will accomplish their mission in the future.

In James Madison's time, our country was largely agricultural and rural. People lived in geographically dispersed areas. Communication was slow and depended largely on the postal service. Individuals lived relatively isolated lives. Since then we have seen the development of the telephone, radio, television, computers, satellites, and much, much more. We have watched the Vietnam War, man landing on the moon, and the potential meltdown of the Three Mile Island nuclear reactor from the comfort of our living rooms.

Technology is making unheard of quantities of information available in undreamed of ways. Recent technological progress includes the development of the computer chip and the optic fiber. According to Jon Roland, in the April 1979 issue of *Futurist*, these developments include:

> . . . by 1985 one will be able to purchase for less than $200 a pocket-size personal computer that is faster and has more memory than the most powerful computer in the world today . . . and by 1985, today's micro-processor will be succeeded by the nano-processor, with a throughput density 1,000 times as great. The pico-processor, with a throughput density one million times as great, will involve circuits on the molecular level and will probably have to be grown rather than constructed under external control.
>
> If a pico-processor could be combined with memory of comparable speed and compactness, and the resulting pico-computer implanted in a person's skull and interfaced with the brain, that person could have more computer power than exists in the world today and all the stored knowledge of humanity as accessible as any brain cell. Such a thing could fundamentally change human nature,

and it is closer to realization than bionic limbs, organs, or senses.

The Information Gap

While these marvels offer the potential that vast amounts of information will be available at the touch of a computer button, at the same time we face the potential of a divided society. This country has always been one of information rich and information poor, but we now face a situation in which that gap could become a chasm, not because we provide any less to the poor, but because technology offers so much more to the rich and the powerful. The spectre of a caste system based on the accessibility of information is a haunting and potent problem with which we must struggle.

As the body of information grows and its transmission becomes more rapid, an individual's need for information has never been greater. Our society has become so complex, with decisions required in so many areas, that ready access to information has become essential to our functioning as individuals or our collective ability to function as a society. A recent report from the Department of Energy concerning the Three Mile Island crisis and the likely results of a meltdown contained the following information:

> Out of a predicted 10 million people who would be exposed to radiation, there would be 3,300 prompt fatalities; 45,000 cases of respiratory impairment and burning of the lung; 240,000 cases of thyroid damage; 350,000 cases of temporary sterility in males; 40,000 to 100,000 cases of prolonged or permanent suppression of menstruation in women; 10,000 to 100,000 cases of acute radiation illness.
>
> As for babies in utero: 100,000 of them would be exposed. All of them could develop cretinism. There might be 1,500 cases of microcephaly—that is, babies born mentally retarded with abnormally small heads.
>
> Fifteen years after the event, we could expect 270,000 cases of cancer and 28,800 thy-

roid tumors and 5,100 genetic diseases. That all adds up to nearly one million so called "health effects."

Citizens must regularly make decisions about where they live, what they eat, what they buy, where they go to school, what jobs they choose to pursue, and who they elect to govern. These decisions require information—information that is or ought to be available at libraries.

Conference Themes

Because access to information is so fundamental to our form of government and so essential to an individual's ability to function in society, the White House Conference will be organized around the various uses of information. The five theme areas are for libraries and information services to meet personal needs; to enhance lifelong learning; to support businesses, organizations, and professions; for governing society; and for international exchange. These themes provide a framework within which important issues may be considered. Throughout, the emphasis will be on the individual information consumer and how he or she can best get the information needed. Some of the issues we expect to be discussed at this conference include:

What legislation is needed to support the distribution of information through library and other information services? What level of cooperation between schools and public libraries is appropriate? Can or should libraries cooperate in some substantive way with public television? Should we establish in this country a forum for continuing debate and discussion about library and information issues? What kind of internal and international standards are necessary to preserve the free flow of information? How can libraries work with other institutions to promote information literacy?

What new and/or traditional forms of preservation are necessary to insure continu-

ing access to information? To what extent can federal information become more available to individual citizens? Is some cooperation between libraries and postal service appropriate, especially in rural areas? What forms of cooperation among libraries and between libraries and other agencies will promote greater access to information? How can the education and training of library and system personnel contribute to the more effective delivery of library and information services?

What kind of balance between privacy and freedom of information is appropriate? What planning and research in developing technology is necessary to ensure continuing access to information? What mechanisms can be employed to heighten public awareness of the need for information and for the opportunities offered by libraries to get that information? What forms of coordination or cooperation among various agencies will promote more effective and efficient delivery of information? What is our national responsibility in providing for the free flow of information between and among countries in the world? How can we as a country support the needs of underdeveloped countries for scientific and technical information?

The fundamental issue that serves as the base for all of our deliberations must be who controls the flow of information. Citizen access to the information and the mechanisms that control its flow is a must.

The Conference Results

But what can a White House Conference accomplish? Clearly, all of the issues listed above and the many hundreds that have been identified in the close to 3,000 resolutions passed at state conferences will not be resolved in four and one-half days of meetings. Our objectives are ambitious but not unrealistic. Hundreds of thousands of people from all across the country have already met in fifty-seven pre-White House Conferences to express their concern for libraries and the people they serve. The political mechanism necessary to accomplish real change is already in place and in operation. Working together, delegates to this conference can realistically hope to achieve the following results:

1. Redefine the operation of libraries in a manner that is consistent with social, technological, economic, and political change.

2. Educate the public about the importance of information in their lives.

3. Publicize the importance of libraries in an information-laden environment.

4. Develop a manageable set of resolutions which will clearly establish priorities and recommend specific action on the part of Congress, the White House, associations, and individuals.

5. Create a well-organized, cohesive, public interest pressure group which will be sensitive to information issues and will be able and willing to lobby for adequate library services.

The Citizens' Lobby

The success of this conference rests initially with its delegates and ultimately with those individuals in our society concerned with the delivery of information. The last objective mentioned above, the formation of a citizens' lobby, is one that is so significant that if it were the only thing to emerge from the conference, the conference would be a success. Clearly, delegates to the conference will discuss many important issues and develop resolutions recommending action, but there must be some citizens' group pushing for the implementation of those resolutions, or they will be lost forever on dusty shelves where reports are usually filed.

Such a group might be composed initially of all delegates, alternates, delegates to state and territorial conferences, librarians, and anyone else interested in libraries and their ability to accomplish their mission in a rapidly changing environment. The organization should function on two levels. First, it should lend support to individuals at the state level and assist in the development of state lobbies. Some states are already well organized, while others might need additional assistance. In any event, the national organization should rest on a strong, well-organized network of state lobbies. Second, the group should coordinate a variety of activities at the national level. Its tasks would include:

- coordinating activity with other related groups, including ALA, ULC, National Friends of the Library, National Citizens Emergency Committee to Save Our Libraries, NCCB, and any other interested groups as appropriate;
- developing and lobbying for specific pieces of legislation that relate to an individual's ability to obtain information;
- monitoring legislation in all related areas, including libraries, information centers, communications and computer innovations, privacy, and freedom of information;
- communicating regularly with members of the group through a newsletter;
- developing new initiatives that are not necessarily legislative; and
- providing research capability regarding possible cooperation among a variety of agencies that provide information to citizens.

Basically, this group would be charged with providing information about information decisions to a wide-ranging group of people. Its goal would be to insure citizens access to the mechanisms that control information flow in this country. The formation of such a group would not only provide for implementation of recommendations, but would also involve a large group of individuals in the continuing process necessary to achieve the kind of library and information services that are essential.

The White House Conference is not a single event. It is a continuing political process. Our goal is to make sure that in an information society we have informed people. This goal can only be realized if we have the dedicated, concerned involvement of citizens and librarians across the country. This goal can be achieved only if we are willing to exercise political power and employ political processes. Now more than ever it is a goal worth striving for. "A popular government, without popular information or the means of acquiring it, is but a prologue to a farce or a tragedy or perhaps both."

6

The Fortune Cookie: Socio-Political Impact of Information Technology

ACHILLES: *Please. Those little cookies look delicious.* (Picks one up, bites into it, and begins to chew.) *Hey! What's this funny thing inside? A piece of paper?*

TORTOISE: *That's your fortune, Achilles. Many Chinese restaurants give out fortune cookies with their bills, as a way of softening the blow. If you frequent Chinese restaurants, you come to think of fortune cookies less as cookies than as message bearers. Unfortunately you seem to have swallowed some of your fortune. What does the rest say?*

ACHILLES: *It's a little strange, for all the letters are run together, with no spaces in between. Perhaps it needs decoding in some way? Oh, now I see. If you put the spaces back in where they belong, it says, "ONE WAR TWO EAR EWE." I can't quite make head or tail of that. Maybe it was a haiku-like poem, of which I ate the majority of syllables.*

TORTOISE: *In that case, your fortune is now a mere 5/17-haiku. And a curious image it evokes. If 5/17-haiku is a new art form, then I'd say woe, O, woe are we. . . . May I look at it?*

ACHILLES (handing the Tortoise the small slip of paper): *Certainly.*

TORTOISE: *Why, when I "decode" it, Achilles, it comes out completely different! It's not a 5/17-haiku at all. It is a six-syllable message which says, "O NEW ART WOE ARE WE." That sounds like an insightful commentary on the new art form of 5/17-haiku.*

ACHILLES: *You're right. Isn't it astonishing that the poem contains its own commentary!*

Reprinted from *Special Libraries*, vol. 72. no. 2, spring 1981, p. 97-102 by Special Libraries Association. Web address (www.sla.org)

TORTOISE: *All I did was to shift the reading frame by one unit—that is, shift all the spaces one unit to the right.*

ACHILLES: *Let's see what your fortune says, Mr. Tortoise.*

TORTOISE (deftly splitting open his cookie, reads): *"Fortune lies as much in the hand of the eater as in the cookie."*

—Douglas R. Hofstadter, *Gödel, Escher, Bach*

Information Technology

In many ways modern information technology can be compared to the fortune cookie in the story. It is a bearer of messages; those messages are frequently ambiguous, and the future clearly lies as much in the hands of those using the technology as it does in the technology itself. Unlike the fortune cookie, however, information technology is radically changing the society in which we live at a rate that is unprecedented. Stanford University economist Edward Steinmuller has noted that if the airlines were progressing as rapidly as this technology, the Concord would be carrying half a million passengers at twenty million miles an hour for less than a penny apiece.[1]

Information technology itself is not new. Computers have been around since Charles Babbage invented the Difference Engine in the mid-nineteenth century, and mankind has been communicating since the beginning of the species. Electronic communication itself has been a fact of life since Morse sent his famous message "What hath God wrought" more than 150 years ago. Little did he know what was to come. There have been quantum leaps in this technology over the past two decades, and the rate of change is expected to continue for at least the next two.

The application of these technologies will ultimately affect every aspect of our lives: the way we work, the way we live, the way we govern ourselves. If we are to design and manage library and information services that will respond to the needs of people in this high-technology environment, it is critical that we examine the social and political changes that flow from technological innovation.

There are many hazards in the business of prophecy. Arthur Clarke has identified two: the failure of nerve and the failure of imagination.[2] The failure of nerve occurs when, given all the relevant facts, the would-be prophet cannot see that they point to an inescapable conclusion. Failure of imagination is more interesting. It arises when all the available facts are appreciated and marshaled correctly—but when the really vital facts are still undiscovered, and the possibility of their existence is not admitted. Leaps of the imagination and discovery have given us such scientific breakthroughs as X rays, nuclear energy, radio and television, photography, sound recording, and transistors. The list goes on.

Today, however, we are in danger of committing a failure of nerve if we fail to carry trends in the application of technology to their logical conclusions. The impact of computer and communications technologies is already apparent. In the United States, 400,000 computers are now doing work that would require five trillion people if done by hand. Moreover, all the information machines in the country can be powered for a year with the energy of one oil tanker, and the primary resource needed to build the machines of the future is sand. In many ways information technology may be considered our new internal combustion engine, driving society in new directions and creating an environment that is in many ways unpredictable.

Howard Resnikoff has called this the era of the fourth great communication invention.[3] The first was the invention of writing about five thousand years ago by the Egyptians and Akkadians. These civilizations flowered as a result of the new-found ability to accumulate knowledge and transmit it from generation to generation. The second was the invention, about three thousand years ago, of the alphabet. The third was the application of movable type to printing in 1453. This invention generated the creation of mass production and dissemination of information at a relatively low cost. In many ways our modern societies can be traced to the invention of movable type. With the advances in telecommunications and microelectronic technology, we find ourselves in the fourth era.

While many may disagree about the speed of application or the extent to which it will affect our society, it is clear that computers are getting smaller, faster, cheaper, more reliable, and more pervasive. The range of applications is growing at an enormous rate. To illustrate the magnitude of change we might consider the human brain as our base. In the early 1950s, it would have taken a computer the size of New York City, and drawing more power than the whole subway system, to contain most of the functional elements of the brain. By the early 1960s, with transistorization, the computer containing those functions had shrunk to the size of the Statue of Liberty, and a 10-kilowatt generator would have kept it going. By the early 1970s, with the introduction of integrated circuits, there had been a further compression down to the size of a Greyhound bus. By the mid-1970s, it was the size of a television set and now is not much larger than a typewriter. Soon, a computer with this capability will shrink below the size of a human brain and will draw all the power it needs from a portable radio battery.

Central to these changes is the silicon chip. At the present time, 100,000 transistors can be integrated on a piece of silicon a quarter-inch square. By 1985, chips containing one million bits are expected to be in use. Computer scientists are even talking about putting thirty million bits on a single chip. By the mid-1980s, a powerful third-generation microcomputer will be available in the $100 price range.

Existing microprocessor techniques can compress information at least ten thousand-fold. The entire contents of a book will soon be found on a single silicon chip that can fit through the eye of a large needle. By the late 1980s, if data compression techniques continue, it will be possible to store an entire library in a space about the size of a paperback. Even now, using video-disc technology read by a laser, it is possible to store the entire contents of the Library of Congress on two hundred feet of shelving, that is, on one wall of a large room. In addition, over five hundred databases are now available online, and additional information, such as the 1980 census data, will be available only in this format.

Breakthroughs in communications systems are closely linked to the development of increased computer capability, creating massive "telecomputing" networks. Digital information may now be transmitted using the electromagnetic spectrum (radio, television, satellite) or some form of telephone line or cable.

Applications of these technologies are almost limitless. Declining costs of both satellite time and earth stations will make possible, in the next few years, the increased use of satellites for video conferencing and interlibrary document transfer. Forecasters estimate that 85 percent of American homes will be on cable by the end of the decade, with many having an interactive capability. In addition, if the telephone company is deregulated, it is likely that subscribers will be offered as many as two hundred channels. Viewdata and teletext systems are bringing massive amounts of information directly into the home, electronic mail is a reality in many places, and a paperless office (perhaps even a paperless library) is on the horizon.

This technology is creating a society in which massive amounts of information can be economically collected, distributed, and controlled. It is creating dislocations not only in traditional institutions but affecting the operation of government, and is generating a host of public policy issues. While many of these issues may seem far removed from our day-to-day activities, their resolution will in fact determine how we live and work in the decades ahead.

Historical Perspective

The United States was founded on the belief that a democratic society depends on an educated and informed electorate. Many of our founding fathers, including Thomas Jefferson, James Madison, and Thomas Paine, spoke eloquently about this principle. Indeed, the belief in diversity of opinion and mobility of ideas is embedded in the First Amendment to the Constitution of the United States.

The Constitution also provided for government involvement in the communication process by granting Congress the power "to establish Post Offices and Post Roads." This early communications network grew slowly but provided the primary means of communication until the introduction of the telegraph in 1837 and the telephone in 1876. The electronic age heralded by these inventions was accompanied by increasing involvement of the federal government in the establishment of what may now be seen as early information policy.

The term "information policy" was not used until the 1970s when a number of organizations and individuals began to build on the earlier work of Fritz Machlup who identified a large, knowledge-based industry in the United States in a landmark study published in 1962.[4] Since then, Daniel Bell has described a coming "post industrial society,"[5]

Marc Porat has concluded after exhaustive research that over 50 percent of the gross national product of the United States is derived from information-related activities,[6] and Alvin Toffler has warned us that we may soon be swept away by "the third wave."[7]

Information Policy Issues

The term "information policy" is best used to describe not a single policy but an interrelated set of policies that condition the availability of information. These policies are concerned with the creation, production, collection, management, distribution, and retrieval of information. Their significance lies in the profound effect they have on the manner in which an individual in society, indeed a society itself, makes political, economic, and social choices.

An analysis of information policy issues, options, and consequences is made more difficult by the fact that information is characterized by a convergence in the technology and a divergence in the use and application of the information itself. Thus, while computer and communications technologies are becoming increasingly indistinguishable, information policy decisions affect energy, transportation, employment, economic development, health, education, international relations, and practically every other program within government. As a result, many informed observers, both within the government and outside it, feel that the primary political issues of the 1980s will be information policy issues.

Several notable attempts have been made to identify the primary issues to be considered. In 1976, the Domestic Council Committee on the Right of Privacy submitted a report to the president of the United States which identified fifteen major issues in five issue clusters.[8] Several years later, in a report that was never published, the National Telecommunications and Information Agency identified seven issue areas.[9] Finally, in 1979 the

Information Industry Association identified some seventy-five issues in nine issue areas.[10]

Many of these issues may be grouped into two general areas of concern: the relationship between information and productivity and a consideration of the role of government and its relationship to the private sector. The first group of issues usually marches ahead under the banner of economy in government, while the second set is concerned in a more straightforward manner with political consequences. The two areas do, of course, interrelate, and both have profound social implications.

Information and Productivity

For years librarians and other information professionals have struggled with the knotty problem of assigning value to information. Whether in communities, businesses, or educational institutions they have sought ways to tell their constituencies what information was worth. To date no satisfactory formula has been discovered, but the subject is now being debated at the federal level.

Within the federal government, the relationship between information and productivity is a subject that is attracting increasing attention. President Carter has established a program to study this relationship within the National Technical Information Service (NTIS), and the Office of Management and Budget (OMB) has issued a series of circulars designed to control the flow of government-generated information and make it more accessible to the public.

Congressman Brooks introduced HR-6410 which resulted in the Paperwork Reduction Act of 1980, approved by the 96th Congress on December 11, 1980, as PL 96-511. The law establishes an Office of Information and Regulatory Affairs within OMB and vests it with considerable power and authority. While this legislation was designed to establish greater efficiency in the management and control of information, many feel that it is a short step from management and control to power and politics. The legislation is to take effect on April 1, 1981.

The rising cost of energy together with the declining cost of communications has generated interest in possible communication/transportation trade-offs. As government and society begin to move information rather than people, certain industrial dislocations are sure to occur. These impacts are already being felt in the automobile and airline industries. Regulatory issues emerge and will become increasingly pronounced in the decade ahead. Massive retraining efforts may become necessary as traditional jobs disappear.

Role of Government

The relationship between the public and private sectors in this country has always been in a state of creative tension. The prominence of information technology has led to a reexamination of regulatory issues and a new look at the degree to which government should intervene in the functioning of the free market. While decisions in this area will have massive ramifications within the United States, they will be even more significant in the international arena. To a large extent the economic position of the United States with respect to the rest of the world depends on the degree to which it exports high-technology and scientific and technical information. While the United States continues to export an increasing quantity of this technology and information, its share of the world market has begun to decline.

As new information packaging and handling capabilities spring up, questions associated with the government's responsibility to protect the public interest proliferate. To what extent should the federal government provide information services that may appear to be competitive with private sector offerings? To what extent is the government obligated to provide information that is unavailable from the private sector in areas such as consumer product safety, employment hazards, or environmental impact? To what extent should information be made available at no cost to the user? What regulatory controls are necessary for emerging technology such as interactive cable? What will be the impact of the new Telecommunications Act when it is finally passed? How can privacy be assured? The answers to these and other questions will surely redefine the role of government in the decade ahead.

In the international information policy area it is commonly felt that there is no agency that speaks for the United States. The Department of State, the International Communications Agency, and the National Telecommunications and Information Administration (NTIA) all have roles, but they are frequently uncoordinated. The World Area Radio Conference held in 1979 illuminated many major issues in this area. The tense relationship between the United States and the underdeveloped countries is reflected in national and world policies governing information distribution and the use of satellite space and other communications technologies.

Conclusion

Resolution of the issues outlined will not be easy. Emerging information technology is radically altering the nature of our society. Over a period of time it is likely to affect the fundamental balance between economic, political, and social value as it exists in our society. It is certain to affect our library and information services, our political structures and institutions, even the basic nature of our government and society.

Technological developments are predictable. Their social and political impacts are not.

We have been given a fortune cookie carrying an often inscrutable message. What we do with that fortune will become the future. For indeed "Fortune lies as much in the hand of the eater as in the cookie."

NOTES

1. Edward Steinmuller is quoted in an article by Thomas O'Toole, "Information Business Booms," *Washington Post,* June 4, 1980.

2. Arthur C. Clarke, *Profiles of the Future* (New York: Harper & Row, 1973).

3. Howard Resnikoff, *Program Report: Information Science and Technology,* National Science Foundation, August 1979.

4. Fritz Machlup, *The Production and Distribution of Information in the United States* (Princeton, N.J.: Princeton University Pr., 1962).

5. Daniel Bell, *The Coming of Post-Industrial Society* (New York: Basic Books, 1976).

6. Marc Porat, *The Information Economy: Definition and Measurement* (Washington, D.C.: U.S. Government Printing Office, 1977).

7. Alvin Toffler, *The Third Wave* (New York: William Morrow, 1980).

8. Domestic Council Committee on the Right of Privacy, *National Information Policy: Report to the President of the United States* (Washington, D.C.: U.S. Government Printing Office, 1976).

9. National Telecommunications and Information Agency, unpublished report.

10. Forest Woody Horton, Jr., ed., *The Information Resource* (Washington, D.C.: Information Industry Association, 1979).

7

Washington Update

A View from the Right

On January 20 Ronald Wilson Reagan will be sworn in as the fortieth president of the United States. This event will mark the second time in four years that the American people have selected a man whose primary qualification for the job is that he has never had a mailing address in Washington, D.C.

Indeed, the ballot box repudiation of all that is Washington extended far beyond the presidential contest. The defeat of congressional stalwarts (and longtime library supporters) such as Warren Magnuson (D-WA), John Brademas (D-IN), Frank Thompson (D-NJ), George McGovern (D-SD), and Jacob Javits (R-NY) shocked many and caused one veteran lobbyist to remark, "It seems that being an incumbent is the greatest liability one can have this year."

As a new, markedly more conservative freshman class of senators and representatives joins the somewhat chastened survivors, it seems likely that President Reagan will have the support he needs to fulfill his campaign pledge to "get the government off our backs."

Washington, filled as it is with intrigue and power mongering, has come to represent the worst of government and in many ways the worst of the governed. But if Washington embodies our greatest fears and deepest suspicions, it also holds our boldest hopes and our loftiest expectations as a people.

And so it is with a combination of expectancy and dread that we prepare to watch the quadrennial ritual that announces the passing of power. In considering the impact of this transition on the future of library programs, we are reminded that there are inexorable laws that dictate and mediate political change just as surely as gravity keeps us from spinning into space. Some of these are:

The Law of Bureaucratic Inertia says that government agencies and programs in motion remain in motion until stopped. Programs that are pending will die unless aggressively promoted.

This law was paramount in the thinking of one Washington official who was asked about the future of library programs: "We will think positive and go ahead. Until the direction is changed, we will continue to run our programs as usual." Others voice the conviction that the Department of Education will remain intact despite campaign rhetoric because it is already in place and its termination would require the consent of Congress.

On the negative side, the force of inertia could impede the passage of the National Library and Information Services and Construction Act when it expires in 1982.

Reprinted from *Library Journal,* January 15, March 15, July, December 15, 1981. Copyright © 1981, Reed Elsevier Inc.

Running contrary to this first law is the Law of Maximum Convergence, also known as the spider web theory. It postulates that in the long run everything touches everything else.

According to this law, it is impossible to increase defense spending, reduce the federal budget, cut taxes at a rate of 10 percent a year for the next three years, and reduce inflation without eliminating some existing programs.

The Law of Political Expediency states that when reducing or eliminating programs, those with less powerful support may be attacked more readily than those with more powerful support.

Finally, there's the Law of Individual Influence. Policy is made by people. Their past performance may indicate their future direction. Thus an examination of Reagan advisors should enlighten us about the new administration's potential position on library programs.

Casper Weinberger, known affectionately as "Cap the Knife," is Reagan's chief budget advisor. Former Secretary of Health, Education and Welfare under Nixon, his views on federal support for libraries are well documented. In 1974, he asserted that "it is appropriate for the administration to consider a diminished federal role in support of libraries."

His position was based on a perceived increase in support for libraries at the state and local levels. While that increase has failed to materialize, and libraries have in fact experienced diminished support, there is no reason to suspect that his fundamental belief that libraries are a local responsibility has changed.

Lorelei Kinder is the Pasadena, California, woman who is directing the transition at the Department of Education. Her experience has been as a political organizer rather than as an educator. While her job is not to set policy but to manage transition, educators were not reassured by her appointment.

The outlook is clearly not brilliant for the immediate future of library programs. In spite of bureaucratic inertia, some programs are sure to bite the dust, and initial indications are that library programs may be among them.

But the situation is not altogether bleak. Many information professionals see a possibility for increased support for research in information technology either through the traditional channels or the Department of Defense. As one policymaker put it: "Information technology is already responsible for 25 percent of productivity gains measured in dollars. If we are to maintain our competitive position in the world market, an investment in research is essential. This could certainly become an area of growth and innovation which libraries could share."

In the waning days of the lame-duck session, Congressman George Brown (D-CA) took a step in that direction by introducing a bill that would establish an Institute for Information Policy and Research which would "address national information policy issues." A key staffer indicated that while the bill is unlikely to pass in its present form, it will be reintroduced in the early days of the new session, and broad bipartisan support is expected for the concept.

A new political era is beginning. Through this column we will monitor developments of special interest to the library community. We will watch the fledgling Reagan administration, report and evaluate appointments, and assess administrative actions.

As the political shell game continues in Congress, we will look for key committee assignments and emerging new leaders that are likely to affect our future. We will take special note of library legislation, but will also monitor the progress of bills dealing with privacy, paperwork reduction, productivity, and telecommunications.

We will listen for trends from the voices of the Heritage Foundation and the Moral Majority, try to determine what "supply-side" economics means to libraries, and see if the Department of Education and National Commission on Libraries and Information Science can avoid the Reagan "hit list."

In short, we will report not only what happens, but also why it happens, who causes it to happen, and what it means to each of us.

The Prisoner's Dilemma

The prisoner's dilemma is a classic model used in game theory to analyze complex economic and social issues. In the problem two men suspected of committing a crime together are arrested and held separately. Each is told that he may either confess or remain silent. If one confesses and the other does not, the one who confesses will be released for turning state's evidence and the other will go to jail for twenty years. If both confess, they both go to jail for five years. If both remain silent, they both go to jail for one year for a lesser crime. The problem for each prisoner is to decide whether to confess or not without knowledge of the other prisoner's decision.

The game provides an appealing analogue for strategists because its essential elements establish the kind of paradox frequently encountered in political decision making. Each player may act either "cooperatively" or "uncooperatively." There is no one "right" solution. When all players act cooperatively, each does better than when all act uncooperatively. For any fixed strategy of one player, the other does better by acting uncooperatively. In every instance it is assumed that each player wishes to maximize his own self-interest.

While we would not wish to imply that Washington has become a prison, the library community is facing a series of dilemmas and decisions that surpasses in number and magnitude anything encountered in the twenty-five-year history of federal support for libraries. The Reagan administration is attempting, as promised, to dismantle a great many government programs, including federal assistance to school libraries, research institutions, and higher education.

Proposals of particular interest to libraries include: consolidation of support for elementary and secondary education into block grants with a total spending reduction of 20 percent. This would virtually eliminate support for school libraries and media centers. It would mean significant reductions in support for higher education and cuts in funding for the National Endowment for the Humanities, the National Science Foundation, and the Corporation for Public Broadcasting, ranging from 25 percent to 75 percent.

Art, culture, and the humanities are out; bombs and other things military are in. The ax-wielding approach to budget cutting seems to rest on the premise that if there is enough blood on the floor, congressional defenders of specific programs can be persuaded to support the reduction program because "all oxen are being gored."

One Washington veteran, assessing the situation, warned against complacency: "Everyone remembers the Nixon days when libraries ended up with more than they started with. That's not what's happening here. There is a different mood in the Congress. We must not delude ourselves with the faith that what worked before will work again."

Jim Rutherford, former Assistant Secretary for Research and Improvement at the Department of Education, reiterated essentially the same message when he spoke to the Legislative Committee of the American Library Association at its Midwinter Meeting. "Any notion of doing anything beyond sustaining where we are is simply not in the cards," he counseled. "The spirit of the country is negative and fearsome. The question is how to hold things together until the mood of the country shifts. The present administration simply reflects that mood."

Speaking as a "private citizen," Rutherford offered some straightforward advice to those seeking to defend library programs. "First," he said, "lie low. Congress and the administration wish to have things to dismember and crush. Avoid visibility." It was a message that was delivered again and again to those with long experience in Washington.

Second, Rutherford maintained that in the long run "libraries are better off with their natural allies, those institutions concerned with knowledge generation, distribution, and use such as museums and research facilities."

Rutherford noted that the library community is often seen as fragmented, a tendency that could prove fatal in the current environment. A congressional staffer emphasized this point as well when she observed, "We don't know what you people want. We want to support libraries, but we get so many different messages."

Clearly, the degree to which libraries can and should cooperate among themselves and with other interest groups is emerging as a major strategy question in the political power game that dominates Washington. Over the next few months library supporters will be concerned with the maintenance of current funding levels, the continuation of administrative structures such as the Department of Education, and the introduction of new legislation to replace the Library Services and Construction Act that expires next year.

Among the major issues: Should library influence be used to help support the current status of the Department of Education, or should it be reserved for specific library funding programs? Is it wise to defend National Endowment for the Humanities and National Science Foundation programs as well as those of the Department of Education? Should the library community push for reintroduction of the National Library and Information Services Act now or wait for a less hostile moment? In each of these instances and in many others that will emerge, the library community must choose its battles with care and form alliances when necessary.

What is at stake in this series of dilemmas is more than federal support for libraries. A way of life, a form of government, social value are at issue. The question is not whether the government tells us what to do or we tell the government what to do. We are the government. It embodies our values as a people. In Jim Rutherford's words, "Why are we having a nation if we can't read a book or go to a play or visit an art museum?"

The stakes are high. The game is messy. The strategy is uncertain. The goal is freedom—but at what cost? It is a dilemma.

Information and Public Policy

Information policy has been variously defined. To some, it is that body of statutes and regulations that governs the telecommunications industry. To others, it is a concern with the issues of privacy and freedom of information. To still others, it is those laws and policies affecting libraries and government printing and publication. All, however, agree that information policy is a rapidly growing, singularly important collection of actions and strategies that affects nearly every aspect of government activity.

In Washington, the information policy discussion has been raised to a new level in this Congress with the introduction of two pieces of legislation. The first, HR 3137, the Information Science and Technology Act of 1981, was introduced on April 8 by Rep. George Brown (D-CA), while Rep. Glenn English (D-OK) introduced HR 1957, the International Communications Reorganization Act of 1981, on February 19.

The "Brown Bill," as it is popularly referred to, would establish an independent Institute for Information Policy and Research "to address National information policy issues; to provide a forum for the interaction of government, industry and commerce, and educational interests in the formulation of National information policy options; to provide a focus and mechanism for planning and coordinating Federal research and development activities related to information science and technology; and to amend the National Science and Technology Policy, Organization, and Priorities Act of 1976 to create a new position of Special Assistant for Information Technology and Science Information."

Specific provisions of the bill call for the transfer to the Institute of the Office of Policy Analysis and Development of the National Telecommunications and Information Agency and any programs specifically concerned with information technology and its impacts in the Division of Policy Research and Analysis of the National Science Foundation; and the establishment of coordination among other government departments and agencies concerned with research and development in the area of information science and technology.

Testifying before the House Committee on Science and Technology in May and June, witnesses were unanimous in their support of the goals of the bill but divided in their assessment of the Institute. Lining up in defense of familiar turf, representatives of government agencies noted that the administration does not support the bill and affirmed their belief that satisfactory research and policy analysis can be accomplished within existing structures.

Tom Galvin, Bob Willard, and Sam Beatty, representing ALA, IIA, and ASIS respectively, found themselves on the same side of an issue, for the first time in recent memory. Each spoke in strong support of the Institute, emphasized the importance of full participation by all stakeholders, and noted the distinction to be made between a central monolithic policy-making agency and the Institute as planned. Galvin avoided using the phrase "information policy" altogether and referred to the need for a "coordinated National information program," while Willard put it more bluntly: "There is an enormous difference between discussing information policy and setting it."

Throughout the hearings, Rep. Brown exhibited a dazzling grasp of the range and complexity of the topic, citing statistics and drawing inferences that amazed and delighted information professionals in the audience.

The bill introduced by Rep. English is also significant though not as controversial as HR 3137. It is based on a report which grew out of four days of hearings held last year by the Subcommittee of the Committee on Government Operations. As a result of exhaustive testimony, the report concluded that: "a critical and expanding set of problems faces the United States in international information flow . . . the current government structure within the executive branch has proven unsatisfactory in responding to existing problems . . . [and] the number and complexity of problems now emerging will be unmanageable within the current governmental structure; past problems will seem minor."

To deal with these problems, the bill would establish a cabinet-level Council on International Communications and Information, which would be responsible for coordinating and reviewing all international communications and information policy. To assist the Council in its work, an Advisory Committee and an Interagency Committee would also be established.

Because this piece of legislation would establish only a coordinating mechanism and not a new agency, it is supported by the administration. It is even rumored that Secretary of State Haig is already moving to have Undersecretary Buckley set up an interagency task force along the lines presented in the bill, but with the Department of State controlling the operation.

Although the focus and structure proposed by the two bills are somewhat different, there are similarities in intent. Both express deep concern about the impact of information on public policy, its role in international negotiations, and its impact on the national economy. Each provides a mechanism whereby public and private sectors can engage in a dialogue concerning important national issues. Each provides a central focus for policy analysis that cuts across departmental lines. Finally, both place responsibility for information policy analysis at a higher level of government.

As noted above, portions of HR 1957 are expected to be implemented in some form. The fate of HR 3137 at a time of government retrenchment is less predictable. Even its most optimistic supporters do not expect to see the bill passed in this Congress. Nevertheless, its long-term importance should not be underestimated. The issues are quite real, and the Institute would accomplish several things that no amount of coordination among existing agencies can be expected to accomplish: it would bring together a critical mass of resources, both human and financial; it would achieve greater visibility at a higher level of government for information policies; and it would establish a central, independent capability for focusing both public and private efforts on solving some of the most important problems of the day. To use one example cited by Rep. Brown, "The improvement of productivity is basically an information issue, but it will probably take most people a little time to realize that."

HR 3137 is a sensible proposal, one that could save our country hundreds of millions of dollars over the long term. Unfortunately, it appears to be ahead of its time.

Research: The Lumber Yard Approach

"Too often the library profession takes what could be called a lumber yard approach to building a house. Our library schools turn out craftspersons and contractors but not architects." This lament was one of many expressed by participants in the recently completed project to develop a Library and Information Science Research Agenda for the 1980s.

The project was the result of a contract issued after competitive bidding by the Department of Education, Office of Libraries and Learning Technologies, to Cuadra Associates. Its purpose was "to assist the Department, and the wider community that it serves, in establishing research priorities for the 1980s in the field of library and information science." It involved the active participation of fifteen "researchers" and eleven "practitioners" who were selected to be broadly representative of the library and information science community.

The centerpiece of the project was a three-day meeting held in the steamy summer ambiance of Airlie House, about fifty miles outside of Washington, D.C. Prior to the meeting each of the researchers had prepared six research projects for discussion, review, and rating, and all participants had made a preliminary evaluation. Nevertheless, participants arrived with some suspicion and a deep sense of humility.

Some questioned the ability of any group, no matter how selected, to arrive at a consensus regarding research priorities; some felt that the group should focus on research areas rather than specific projects; some were uncomfortable with ranking projects which were not fully developed. Many were aware that previous efforts in research agenda building had met with limited success. A discussion of evaluation criteria revealed many differences in priorities among the participants themselves, with some concentrating on goals and objectives while others were more concerned with methodology.

No effort was made to reconcile differences in approach. Participants were instructed to use any criteria that made sense and to discuss projects and concerns openly. At the conclusion of the meeting, however, the group was expected to produce a list of twenty priority projects. The final list of twenty contains those projects which the group felt to be the most significant areas for research in the coming decade. Some of the projects included remained as originally written. A few were written at the meeting as concerns were refined. Several combined aspects of preliminary projects.

Those projects making the "top twenty" were in the following areas:

1. *Information Generation and Provision of Library and Information Services.* This section includes four projects: two concerned with the electronic generation, storage, and delivery of information, and two dealing with the development of automated reference services.

2. *Information Users and Uses.* Although many participants felt that users have been over-studied, others argued persuasively that some user groups have in fact been overlooked. Thus three projects concerning information needs, two about information-seeking behaviors, and four analyses of information access and use were among the twenty projects on the final list, making this the largest single general area.

3. *Economics of Information and of Library and Information Services.* Another large area, economic and financial issues, is the subject of five projects on the list. One is designed to determine costs of library and information serv-

ices, one explores alternative funding possibilities for publicly supported library and information services, and three examine the economic value of information.

4. *Education and Professional Issues.* This section contains only one project which deals with the dissemination and diffusion of library and information science research and practice.

5. *Intellectual Freedom.* The one project included here deals with an examination of groups which promote censorship in public libraries and schools.

This list of projects is clearly not complete. For a variety of reasons, some areas in which serious research is needed are not included. Some of these are education and training, preservation, and use of technologies in the workplace. Other familiar topics such as networking issues were not included because many of the participants felt that the area had been researched enough and needed something more in the way of implementation.

As the meeting moved inexorably toward its conclusion, participants voiced increasing concern about the nature of research and its communication and use. One practitioner expressed this mounting concern eloquently: ". . . I would like to see more discussion about how to improve communications and the dissemination of information in terms of what's going on in research versus the world at the firing line. I'm appalled at how underinformed I am about research going on in the field."

At the final session participants reflected on the agenda. Some felt "satisfied, pleased with the results." Others noted that it was "not complete," and needed to be augmented by other efforts. One researcher felt that there was "not enough weight on conceptualization," and another was "disappointed in the lack of risk taking."

There are those who feel that the Research Agenda in its final form lacks specificity, does not contribute to the resolution of management problems, and is too ambitious. There are others who see it as too pedestrian and not forward looking enough.

In the final analysis, its value will most likely depend on the degree to which it either opens or closes vistas. If it stimulates interest in research and a creative approach to problem solving, it will have been a success; but if it sets boundaries and prevents the emergence of additional issues, it will impede progress.

The Agenda itself is a political document, and could be nothing else. Participants were selected to represent diverse interests, and interaction was characterized by a sensitivity to the needs of competing interest groups. There are inventive projects to be sure, but there is also a little something for everyone. Extremes were eliminated in the interest of balance.

This does not diminish the importance of the effort. Our profession needs such rational, well-balanced, political approaches to questions of universal interest. It needs to build constituent support for activities as critical as research. But it also needs to nourish the dreamers and visionaries who topple convention and upset balance to create a new order.

The Research Agenda is a good lumber yard approach. The materials, the people, and the systems necessary for change are all included. All we need now are the architects.

8

Politics and the Public Library: A Management Guide

As I was preparing for this presentation, a colleague in Cleveland asked what I was going to say. "I think I'll try telling the truth," I responded. She looked at me for a long moment and finally commented, "Well, you might be able to get away with it. You'll be out of town."

Those of us who operate libraries, or other public institutions, for that matter, are not accustomed to getting away with much of anything. In fact, most of us find that our jobs are not well understood by many people either inside or outside the library profession.

Just recently my mother finally worked up the courage to ask, "What exactly is it that you do? I know what your title is, but what do you do when you go to work?" It's a sensible question. Nevertheless, it made me think in a different way about the job of a public library director, and I have come up with the following explanation.

Steady As She Goes, Mr. Sulu

I fight the Klingons. After all, if you remember your *Star Trek,* Scotty actually runs the ship. Captain Kirk sets the direction and fights the Klingons. Of course, he also keeps Dr. McCoy and Spock working together, and communicates with Star Fleet Command, but

his primary job is to keep the ship on course and moving toward its goal in spite of problems that may arise.

In a political environment there seem to be plenty of Klingons to deal with. Funding obstacles, governance issues, personnel limitations, and press relations are chief among them. When I was hired to run the White House Conference on Library and Information Services some years ago, a colleague took me aside and gave me some friendly advice. "The job is impossible," he said. "You have no control over your budget, you can't hire or fire your employees, and your goals are set by elected officials. It's like walking into a boxing match with a blindfold and one hand tied behind your back. Survival is about the best you can hope for."

My experience then, and since then, has convinced me that while my advisor's caution may have been justified, he was overly cynical in his conclusion. It is true that public institutions operate within a world of especially challenging constraints and relationships. But it is equally true that these same conditions and relationships can be managed productively, for the good of the institutions and in the best interests of the people the institution serves.

Politics in this context refers not to partisan politics but to the more generic art of influencing government policy. While the management of any organization is political to the extent that one must try to influence decision makers, and I trust that some comments will resonate with colleagues in academic and private sector environments, public libraries deal directly with government. Indeed, one might argue that public libraries are part of government.

This governmental context brings with it some special conditions. Governance of a public library is most often through a Board of Trustees; funding is typically a function of the political process and as such it is neither constant nor predictable; employment practices are regulated either by Civil Service rules or union contracts; and the press is an ever-present factor in day-to-day operations. In addition, goal setting must be done in conjunction with local elected officials and negotiating skills provide the glue that holds it all together.

Governance and the Board of Trustees

There are a number of governance structures for public libraries. Some public libraries are departments of city or county government and have no Board of Trustees at all, or only an advisory board. Other public libraries are departments of city or county government and have a policy-making board as well. A third type of public library governance occurs when the library operates as an independent, not-for-profit corporation, with or without independent taxing authority. Finally, there are a few public library systems that are part of state government.

The power of a Board of Trustees varies enormously, depending on the role of the board within the governmental structure and the strength of the individuals on the board. An advisory board has little direct power. It cannot set policy. It cannot allocate resources. It does not hire or fire the director. Indirectly, such a group can bring terrific pressure to bear on policymakers, and many advisory boards are fine advocates for libraries, but they are limited by their inability to set policy

directly. Still, an advisory board is better than no board at all.

A policy-making board for a library located structurally within government has the toughest and most ambiguous role of all. Charged with setting policy, a board in this situation is constrained by its inability to generate and allocate funds. Without this implementing capability, the board is restricted realistically to making policy decisions about nonfiscal library programs and activities. This type of board is more powerful than an advisory board. It can hire or fire the director. It can take definitive stands on issues of intellectual freedom. It can approve long-range plans and recommend budgets to elected officials. It cannot, however, prevent the governing body from freezing staff, closing facilities, or reducing funds available for the purchase of materials.

Library boards governing libraries that are independent, not-for-profit institutions have the highest level of power. This type of board exercises power comparable to that available to the board of a corporation. It can hire or fire the director. It can make policy on nonfiscal issues. It can even allocate resources. Within budgetary constraints it can open or close facilities, expand or contract the staff, increase or decrease the budgetary allocation available for materials. Financial resources available to the library remain within the library. They are not vulnerable to reallocation to other city or county departments.

There are two secrets to the development and maintenance of a productive working relationship with a Board of Trustees: clear role definition and the communication of adequate and appropriate information.

A public library is just that, the public's library. It belongs to the citizens of a given community. It does not belong to the library director. Trustees are selected as representatives of the community to govern the library. The library director is hired by those trustees to manage the institution and to carry out policies established by the board. The board makes policy. The director carries out policy.

As straightforward as this principle may seem, many of the problems that arise between directors and boards are a result of a confusion of roles. Either the director tries to set policy or the board tries to manage the institution. The scenario that most often develops is one in which the director begins to feel that he or she is better able to make policy decisions than the board. A series of conflicts develops. The board, deprived of its ability to make policy, begins to try to control the director by managing the institution. By moving too far into the establishment of policy the director creates a vacuum that is filled by trustees who are frustrated in their attempts to perform their own jobs.

The director's job goes beyond the simple implementation of policy. It is also the responsibility of the director to make sure that trustees have all the information they need to make informed decisions. This includes background information about the community, board information about national library trends and issues, and specific information concerning the issue under discussion. With respect to information needed to make specific decisions, bulk is not necessarily better.

Appropriate information may be an analysis of cost and benefits or a comparison of options clearly and concisely presented. It may also be a phone call to let an individual trustee know about a pending problem or a possible call from the press. At the most fundamental level, good decisions are based on complete, comprehensive, timely information.

Funding

The operating budget for all public libraries (with the partial exception of the New York Public Library's Research Libraries) comes from tax-generated revenues. Sometimes, as in the state of Ohio, library support is a combination of state-collected income tax and local property tax. Most often public libraries receive a portion of local property tax that is collected and allocated on a year-to-year basis by city or county government.

No matter how revenues are collected or allocated, public libraries are constantly confronted with the twin political realities of the public's aversion to taxes and the need to compete with other public agencies, many of which do good, for a reasonable share of the pie. The goal, then, is to find effective ways to get and keep an adequate budget in a volatile, pressure-filled environment.

The political strategies for achieving this goal include the provision of the highest quality service possible, the effective presentation of budget requests, an understanding of political pressure points, and the ability to mobilize an effective demonstration of power.

In poll after poll across the country, citizens rank public libraries at or near the top of all public agencies in the importance of the service they provide and their success in providing it well. Nevertheless, budgets continue to be inadequate. That reality indicates that there must be more to the decision-making process than logic would suggest. Still, libraries must continue to make every effort to maintain that level of performance. It is a necessary, but insufficient, condition for achieving adequate support.

The first point at which showmanship comes into play is at the initial presentation of the budget. Many of us have learned that a picture is indeed worth a thousand words and have come to rely on graphs, charts, and cartoons from the *New Yorker.*

I remember several years ago making a budget presentation during a year of austerity. The mayor had directed all departments to reduce their budget by some percentage. The library board directed me to go forward with a proposed budget that was an increase. When we appeared before the appropriate committee we presented a pie chart with the library's slice of .5 percent of total revenues indicated. As you can imagine it looked a lot like a straight line. What we said was, "Where are you going to make a reduction, and, if you do, what difference will it make anyway?" We got our increase.

I don't mean to suggest, however, that a

flashy presentation will solve all your financial problems. I have made equally splendid presentations with the opposite result. Presentation is, after all, only a continuation of a logical process, and politics is a function of power. The elements that are most useful in acquiring political support for the library budget are an understanding of political pressure points, and the willingness and ability to lean on them.

If the library budget is to be approved by seven elected officials, you need four votes. The way you get those votes may vary. Individual telephone calls from a few well-placed supporters may persuade some, while others may be more affected by the two hundred library supporters who pack the hearing room. No one strategy is always right. The point is you have to know the pressure points and develop a strategy that is appropriate to the situation.

Personnel Management

Just as with the section on funding, this is not meant to be a full discussion of personnel management. Comments are restricted to those issues that have some political component.

Conventional wisdom tells us that public agencies have limited control over personnel, that civil service rules and regulations and union contracts make it impossible to manage. In fact, just the opposite is true.

Civil service was instituted to counteract the abuses of patronage. Its goal was the establishment of a system in which individuals would be hired and promoted on the basis of merit. In fact, what civil service has accomplished is the removal of personnel issues from the political process.

Unions representing public employees have done much the same thing. By focusing on the development of fair labor practices and adequate levels of compensation, they have served to protect staff from the more damaging aspects of politics. While we must acknowledge the fact that unions are themselves political in a broader sense, and may in fact assist libraries in funding strategies described above, their goal is to depoliticize the workplace.

The largest remaining political issue in the personnel area is the achievement of adequate compensation for library employees. Although this issue surely has a large impact on library staff, it can most appropriately be seen as a funding issue.

The Fourth Estate

Contrary to popular opinion, the press is not the enemy. Successful press relations depend on a recognition of the fact that an organized approach to press relations is an important part of management's job and an understanding of how the press operates and what reporters are trying to achieve.

At the most basic level, a reporter is trying to write—or film or record—a good story. Print reporters have a designated number of column inches to fill while television or radio reporters fill time segments, generally very short time segments. You can help reporters do their job better by providing quotable quotes and good photo opportunities. If you are trying to increase media coverage of the library, sensitivity to what is considered newsworthy will build credibility with working journalists.

In conjunction with this, an understanding of how the press and media operate will also contribute to good press relations. Everyone has a deadline. For most morning dailies that deadline is generally around 7:30 P.M. While pressing stories can come in later, library items are usually not that urgent. If you want press coverage of board meetings and major announcements, it makes sense to schedule them at a time when they can be covered. Some libraries have even been known to change the time of their board meetings to fit in with press deadlines.

Timing is important with TV news also. If you want to be on the 6 P.M. news you should schedule your events between 11 A.M. and 3 P.M. Noon is always good. You might begin to notice how many news events seem to happen around noon. Sometimes a TV station will arrange for live coverage, but unless you have a real emergency on your hands such coverage would be scheduled in advance.

The 11 P.M. news on Sunday has the highest ratings of the week. In addition, there is often little hard news available. Many libraries are open on Sunday and are often quite busy. You might consider showcasing a program or making an announcement early on Sunday afternoon. Just make sure that it's more than talking heads. You will reach a lot of people and make some TV reporters happy in the process.

Don't wait until you have a problem or a message to deliver to establish good press relations. Open communication, which is the basis for trust and rapport, should be developed early on. I remember one time in Atlanta when we were generating a long-range plan for the Atlanta Public Library. At each stage in the planning we met with members of the editorial board of the *Atlanta Journal Constitution* to explain what we were doing and to answer any questions the board members might have.

When the time came for citizens to vote on the $38 million bond referendum we once again packed up our charts and graphs and answers and went down to ask for the endorsement of the newspaper. The group of editors asked us a single question: Is this the same plan you've been talking about for the last two years? When we said yes, they agreed to endorse the referendum with no further discussion.

Choosing a Spokesperson

Who should speak to the press? While there is no single answer to the question, there are some principles upon which I have come to rely. In Cleveland, our public relations officer handles most of the day-to-day contacts with the press. She has developed her contacts, and in many instances real friendships, over a period of years. Newspaper and media representatives have come to know and respect her. She is the first person to be called if an is-

sue arises. She fields the questions and refers them to appropriate individuals for response.

If the question or story is about a library service, the staff member most knowledgeable is asked to respond. We feel that the most knowledgeable person is the best representative of the library and do not try to restrict press contact. Thus, a children's librarian will discuss the latest children's program, the head of special collections answers questions about our rare book acquisitions, and branch librarians talk about service in their neighborhoods.

If the issue is a broad one, or a highly sensitive one, the director talks with the press. Some examples of such issues are increases or decreases in service, library policy regarding privacy of library records, long-range plans, or the impact on the library of an increase or reduction of the library's budget.

There are some situations that are so sensitive that it is usually in the best interests of the library for the president or chair (titles vary) of the board to respond to press inquiries. Major changes in service, policy, or direction fall in this category. The closing of a branch or the initiation of a major capital campaign are some examples of this type of issue.

In all dealings with the press there are several things to keep in mind. There are the three rules of press relations: (1) always tell the truth; (2) never volunteer information; and (3) never speculate.

The first rule is obvious. You simply must deal honestly with the press if you expect them to be fair and honest with you. This includes, by the way, notifying the press about newsworthy items in a timely fashion.

Obviously, rule number two does not apply to those instances when you are trying to generate press coverage. What it does refer to is the management of a crisis situation. If a branch has been closed and the newspaper, radio, and television have all sent out reporters to cover the events, they might ask a staff member how the public is reacting. Staff members should answer the question honestly, but should not go on to compare this problem with one they experienced two weeks ago. That kind of thoughtless response can lead to stories that might be damaging. Moreover, they are irrelevant to the story being covered.

Speculation can generate exciting copy but it is almost never factual and can be gravely misleading. Questions that begin, "How do you think Mr. Jones feels?" or "What do you think Mrs. Smith thinks?" or "What do you think will happen next?" all lead the responder into a line of speculation that may indeed have no basis in fact. None of us really knows what someone else thinks or feels. We can only report on actions.

A final word about the press. I will always remember what I call the Kissinger Doctrine (having first been enunciated by Henry Kissinger). It states that whatever is going to come out eventually should be disclosed immediately. Most of us don't deal with state secrets, but occasionally encounter a situation that we'd rather not disclose to the press. Remember, if it's that big a problem, it's probably going to come out anyway. If you disclose the potentially embarrassing information, it is less likely to be embarrassing.

Care of Elected Officials

Elected officials often get a bad rap. While it is true that some politicians use public office for private gain or abuse the public's trust in some other way, it is equally true that there are numerous elected officials who take their responsibilities seriously and work long and hard to improve government and the services government provides. In working with elected officials it helps to begin by assuming that most are competent and committed. It also helps to understand the goals and constraints that influence their decision-making processes.

Elected officials, without exception, have a broad agenda and numerous constituents. Libraries are seldom at the top of their list of concerns. Libraries are, however, well thought of in most communities and elected officials are happy to support them, especially if they become a part of a larger agenda. Since most public libraries have a great many needs, it is usually not difficult to tie one or more into the overall agenda of the community.

A few examples may help illustrate this point. If a given community is deeply concerned with neighborhood development or redevelopment, the library might want to emphasize its branch services and the contributions that branch libraries make to the neighborhood. If, on the other hand, the community is focused on downtown development, it would be an appropriate time to examine the role of the main library in supporting business growth and to propose needed improvements of the main library facility. Some elected officials are interested in brick and mortar programs while others are more concerned with services. In any event, most will be more likely to support the library actively if it is sensitive to the overall directions of the community.

That is not to say the library is not an important force in itself. Anyone who has had to close a branch library knows that libraries are one of the most important positive elements in any community. Not only do they provide important services on a regular basis, but they are also a symbol of knowledge, of wisdom, and the possibility of progress for individuals and for the community. However an individual elected official may feel personally about the contributions of the library, few can ignore the importance of this institution to voters.

Rules for working with elected officials are similar to those suggested for working with the press. Relations should be developed early on, before a situation arises that requires political assistance, and formal and informal channels of communication should be developed and maintained. In Cleveland, we send a personal letter and report on library activities every month to all elected officials in the area, whether we think we will need their help or not. In addition, we make a point of notifying appropriate elected officials when any important library-related activity is planned for a specific district.

If you do need help in a specific situation, don't assume that the individual you are approaching is fully aware of the details, no matter how many times they may have been in the newspaper. Be prepared to provide a clear, straightforward briefing. If you want help, be prepared to ask for the specific action you need. "We just want your support on this issue" is too vague. If you want a vote, ask for it. If you want an individual to make a phone call, have the number ready. Most elected officials have limited time for any one issue. Use the time you have with them effectively.

For elected officials, timing is a critical element in any decision. Remember that elected officials are *elected*. If you can avoid it, don't ask one to take an unpopular position in an election year. Libraries want to avoid any kind of involvement in partisan politics, but that does not mean that we should be naïve about the conditions under which elected officials work.

Negotiating Strategies

Negotiation is the glue that holds everything together in a political environment. Negotiating strategies include timing, pacing, and presentation. Negotiating skills are more specific than simple communications skills and are useful in all of the relationships described above. In this section I will simply list some strategies and observations that I have found useful over the years:

Pacing in organizational development is critical. Typically, there should be a pushing forward followed by an easing off. This gives both the community and staff the opportunity to assimilate change. No organization can sustain the stress of unremitting progress. Sawtooth development is natural and healthy.

It is almost impossible to expand and contract an institution at the same time. The strategies and rhetoric are different. Unfortunately, many public libraries have had far more experience with contraction than they have had with expansion. Still, there are benefits that can be gained in lean times. Cutting from one area to add to another, however, may be good management, but it is political quicksand.

One goal of management is to make whatever happens an asset. Anyone can play a good hand; it takes skill to play a mediocre hand. Nowhere is the imperfection of life more obvious than in the falling apart of well-laid plans. Examples are numerous. The situation may involve the starting up of a new service, increase in the operating budget, or the negotiation of a major contract. In any case you may have planned carefully only to be confronted by some change or obstacle. You may lose the vote of a key elected official. Perhaps your Board of Trustees voted differently from the way you expected. Your project will fare far better if you incorporate the change or unexpected action into your overall approach than if you bemoan the loss of your original plan of action.

Never overlook the possibility that they may be right. In conflict situations most of us assume that our position is the correct one. That is not always the case. Sometimes a different perspective brings with it an important insight.

Timing is crucial. Don't try to rush things; let the situation mature. Remember it takes nine months to have the baby whether you have one woman or nine working on the project. Process is important. Let the situation fully expand before trying to solve the problem. A quick solution is not always the best solution.

Always control the space of a debate, the context in which decision making will take place. Most people will decide among alternatives presented to them. If you present alternatives, any one of which is satisfactory, you will be likely to achieve your goal without alienating needed support.

Stick to facts, not an interpretation of facts. Try to avoid assigning motives to people, especially elected officials, staff, and the press. You will almost always be wrong, and it won't help your cause anyway.

Reduce the debate to a few easily understood points. This is especially important if a crisis becomes public. Examples include the closing of a branch, a strike by a union, or an attempt to pass a levy or bond referendum.

There are four stages in a negotiation: (1) posturing; (2) smoke; (3) personal attacks; and (4) resolution. Pumping smoke is a strategy that is usually used by people when their case is weak and not supported by the facts. Personal attacks, though distasteful, are usually a sign that the end of a dispute is near. They represent an act of desperation.

Pacing in negotiations is like a marble in a sink. The tempo quickens as the solution nears. Contract negotiations are classic. They generally begin with interminable discussions that appear to accomplish very little, but end with a great deal concluded in a limited amount of time.

Remember the rule of three: when an individual has a list of problems or issues, the third is always the most important one.

Share the glory. When there is credit, there is always plenty to go around.

"I understand how you feel." These words are magic, but only if you really mean them. By affirming the emotional response of an individual to a given situation, you can often move on to a discussion of the facts of the matter. Without the initial affirmation, progress is often impossible.

Functions of a PL Director

Running a library in a political environment is a challenging but not impossible task. Fortunately there are many skilled library directors in communities of all sizes that thrive on the conditions described. While there are many definitions of leadership, I like to think of it as a combination of vision, courage, stamina, and the ability to communicate effectively.

Vision is needed to set the goals. Courage is needed to fight the Klingons. Communications skills are needed to get and keep needed support. But stamina is the quality that makes it all possible. After all, when you go back to City Council for the sixth time on the same issue, it isn't vision that keeps you going.

After reviewing this document, a colleague noted that my observations are too upbeat. He said that I appear to overlook the possibility that some members of the press might really distort the news, that elected officials are sometimes hostile, and that trustees are occasionally unsupportive.

While all of that is true, managing in a political environment is nothing more or less than working with people. Each individual has different sets of goals and values but most try to accomplish good, as defined in very personal terms. These goals and values may not duplicate our own but they are not necessarily in conflict with them. We are more likely to achieve respect and understanding for ourselves and our institutions if we begin with respect and understanding for the people with whom we come in contact.

As we lead our libraries through the force-fields of competing interests, it is important for us to keep in mind that all aliens are not enemies, some are allies. Our goal is to work with trustees, elected officials, the press, and others in our communities to find a shared path to the public good.

PART III

Innovation

Innovation is the process whereby an "institution interacts with its environment and in doing so changes internally." It is "the lifeblood of any institution" because "either an institution changes in response to its environment or it dies." Libraries, like other institutions, both public and private, are changing, sometimes more rapidly than they find comfortable. This section takes the need to innovate more or less for granted and concentrates on strategies for creating innovation and not just change. Change alone can be positive or negative but has a whimsical quality about it, while innovation builds on solid institutional goals based on a regular and continuing awareness of the public we serve.

In reading these chapters, several questions suggest themselves:

- Why innovate?
- When do you innovate?
- How do you bring about positive institutional change?
- When should a library not change?

This last question reminds me that, like efficiency, innovation in the pursuit of the wrong goal is no achievement. As is true in so many things, balance is the key.

9

Managing Innovation

On the evening of January 16, 1991, war broke out in the Persian Gulf. By 10 A.M. the next morning the Cleveland Public Library was offering complete Associated Press (AP) wire service reports about Operation Desert Storm via the library's dial-up information service, which is available to anyone using any of the six hundred terminals in the eighteen library systems throughout northern Ohio, as well as to anyone in a home, office, or dorm with a computer terminal and a modem.

This event is significant not because of the technology involved—the library's twenty-four-hour, seven-days-a-week dial-up service has been developing for the last two years—but rather because it represents the library's innovation in predicting patron need and responding fast. When building the dial-up service (which includes access to the shared catalog of the Cleveland Public Library and seventeen other library systems; the most current subject/title/author index available from any library in the United States to articles in more than 1,400 magazines; and a union list of periodicals available in more than sixty business, university, and medical libraries in a local five-county region), the library learned to experiment and to forge partnerships with vendors to keep improving service. Engaged in this dialog, the library

knew to contact Dow Jones News/Retrieval World Report and ask for two weeks of free access to AP news reports right as the Persian Gulf crisis hit. Dow Jones, as a public service, agreed to do so.

By responding so promptly, the library received the highest patron praise: increased use. In the two weeks of free AP news reports, use of the dial-up service doubled—staff and patrons in libraries throughout the Cleveland area clustered around video display terminals minutes after each new report appeared, office-bound workers without access to regular media reports thanked the library for its sensitivity to their needs and concerns.

Interactive Innovation

Innovation is the lifeblood of any institution. It is an organic process, almost biological in the sense that the institution interacts with its environment and in doing so changes internally. These changes are reflected in services given back to the environment. The process is interactive and continuous. Either an institution changes in response to the changing needs and opportunities of its environment or it dies. Stasis is slow death.

The astonishing speed with which the library provided information about the Gulf war was a direct result of innovative thinking on the part of half a dozen library employees working in four different departments, and systems and partnerships that have been built up over many years. These people reflect a shared understanding of the role of the library, the ability and willingness to communicate internally and externally with those organizations necessary to the success of the project, and a conviction that the project could work.

Libraries are not unlike other organizations in their need to innovate. Many of the examples found here are technological innovations because technology offers the most obvious and dramatic opportunity for change. Technology does not exist in a vacuum, however, and technological change creates and responds to other dimensions of change within an organization.

The use of technology in any organization goes through three stages that we may think of as substitution, extension, and innovation. In the substitution phase, automated systems are used to replace processes previously performed manually. In the extension phase, new services are developed that simply could not be provided at all without automation. Finally, the combination of automated old systems and new capabilities brings about a reshuffling within the institution that we may think of as a redesign of the role of the institution as a whole and its relationship to its environment.

Libraries begin using automation to assist with internal operations. Cataloging, circulation, inventory control, and the ordering of materials are good examples of library functions that are usually automated in this first substitution phase. Once these functions are automated, libraries may begin to provide remote access to their electronic catalogs and use telecommunications systems developed to provide access to other databases and gateways to still others. This extension phase cuts across the previous limitations of time and space in the delivery of information and information services. One might argue that the library becomes less a warehouse and more an access point.

Which brings us naturally to our third stage, innovation, or a reevaluation of the role of the library within the community it serves and, by extension, the appropriate distribution of resources within the library. This is not to suggest that the stages flow freely and distinctly, or that the question of role definition is something that is settled abruptly or decisively like the turning of a page or the closing of a book. In fact, all three stages of development are likely to be found at the same time in a single institution, with role redefinitions proceeding slowly as technological capabilities are weighed against traditional function and changing community need.

Partnerships with the Outside

If there is one word that most accurately describes what is needed for libraries to provide innovative services in a highly technological environment, that word is partnerships. Partnerships with electronic publishers (a term I am using in its broadest sense to include software producers as well as database publishers) are necessary for the collection of information, and partnerships with other libraries and institutions are useful in the distribution of information.

It was only through contact with Dow Jones that the Cleveland Public Library was able to provide those AP wire service reports of the war in the Gulf. Even more significant, however, are the partnerships with Data Research Associates (DRA) and Information Access Company (IAC) that have enabled the library to be the test site for dial-up access to the indexing of 1,400 current journal titles; the cooperative relationship with OCLC that allows us to provide access to sixteen million titles worldwide; and the understandings with other libraries that make it possible for us to provide gateway access to their collections. These partnerships are significant because they transcend the conventional relationships between vendor and customer. They make it possible for us to experiment with new services with minimal risk.

Libraries cannot only be the testing ground for new technologies but also for the other issues raised by them. As we move toward full-text delivery and dial-up access to large information databases, for example, our greatest challenge will be to find an interpretation of copyright that protects publishers while allowing libraries to make full use of electronic storage and retrieval capabilities. Current conflicts with respect to copyright of electronic information arise as libraries and publishers alike try to predict the potential result of any new approach. Each fears to establish a precedent that may ultimately undermine it. Cooperative experimentation provides us with a mechanism for testing the impact of approaches such as the use of licensing agreements. By measuring impact in the controlled experiment of testing a new product at a library, publishers, libraries, and users can gain experience and may be able to make more informed judgments.

These new electronic capabilities also build on the function of the conventional print-based libraries. We expand our work partnership with publishers to include electronic publishers, and we also work with an expanded distribution system through branches, affiliated libraries, and dial-up access.

Technology does not replace a conventional library, it complements it. Emerging electronic libraries appear to be providing access to print collections housed locally and remotely, while providing direct access to the full text of other material that is stored, and sometimes even created, electronically.

Five Rules for Innovation

Just as the relationship of the library to its environment requires partnerships, innovation within the institution itself requires the establishment of attitudes and systems that recognize and reward creativity. These are presented below as five rules for innovation. They are not meant to be exhaustive, but are the minimum prerequisites for institutional creativity.

1. Develop a shared vision. If any institution hopes to be innovative in achieving its mission, it must have a pretty good idea what

that mission is. No amount of institutional wiring will replace a shared vision. No management chart, no committee, no directive will replace constant internal debate and discussion. Questions like: "What are we trying to achieve?" and "How does this contribute to that goal?" must be part of every discussion about new services and even old ones. An institution that recognizes the interplay between change and stability and encourages staff to think about options is one that will respond quickly to new opportunities.

Part of this shared vision may be characterized as an imaginative understanding of users' needs. If a library defines its role in terms of goals rather than means for achieving those goals, technology is seen more as an opportunity and less as a threat. Thus a reference librarian, realizing that an important goal of the library is to provide good information fast, will suggest making AP wire service reports available to the staff and to the public.

2. Communicate, communicate, communicate. The bridge between an organizational structure of any type and the need for innovative solutions to complex problems is communication—frequent, formal, and informal communication across lines of authority. In discussing any new venture the first question must be: Is everyone here that needs to be here? The automation department cannot develop reference support services without talking to the reference librarians. At the same time the ability to implement is a requirement for any good idea. If lines of communication are open and flexible, it makes it possible for that reference librarian with the good idea to say "what if," and find out directly from the automation department if the idea can be implemented, and from the administration if it is legal.

3. Empower employees to make a difference. The real strength of an organization lies not at the top, but in the middle. Teachers carry on the primary work of schools; doctors and nurses are the backbone of hospitals; and librarians carry on the business of answering questions of their constituents. Innovation often begins with those in most direct contact with users of the library. But good ideas are never enough. It's too easy to come up with a solution to someone else's problem. The real challenge is to come up with a better way to do your own job.

Because so many jobs and so many problems overlap, communication across lines is essential. At the same time there must be accountability. When a committee leaves the table, each person must know what he or she is responsible for accomplishing. This implies that employees believe that things can and should happen, and that they will be held responsible for their part of the project. Innovation without an operational level of accountability will remain only a dream.

4. Take limited risks. This rule is especially important in the use of technology. Too often organizations think they need to make a go/no-go decision when a little judicious experimentation would provide a sounder base for a final decision. New uses of technology almost always bring surprises. Sometimes they are more pleasant than others, but there are few instances in which we have not been surprised about something. By trying out a new service on a limited basis, the library commits a relatively small amount of money to the project and is able to adapt and amplify as needed.

5. Use technology, don't invent it. While we at the Cleveland Public Library are very aggressive about the use of technology—we try all sorts of things, experimenting left and right—we are also very clear about this rule. Public libraries are not funded to do much in the way of research and development. Moreover, there is a lot of available technology that we are only beginning to exploit.

Another way to put this is: when you're on the cutting edge of technology, stay on the right side of the blade.

PART IV

Economic Issues

Economics is a continuing force in contemporary society. Just as with other public institutions, libraries tend to do well in economic good times and suffer from budgetary cuts in bad times. Although billed as a discussion of user fees, the primary thrust of the two articles in this section is a consideration of the principles of economic theory and municipal finance, especially as they apply to the delivery of library services. Although the data are obviously dated, the principles discussed are still valid and still important. The articles include definitions of public and private goods, the significance of spillover effects, and an explanation of the benefit received principle. Additionally, the articles acknowledge the close interrelationship between economic and political arguments for the provision of public goods and services. This mingling of economics and politics continues today, with one often masquerading as the other.

In reviewing the articles, I was struck by one dramatic change in the role of libraries. Public libraries are no longer "poorly used," although we might argue that they are still "inadequately supported." The explosion over the last few years of Internet access from public libraries has dramatically changed the public perception of the library. People now come not only for books, but also for information. Computer searching, either on-site or remotely, now dwarfs the circulation of books as a public service, and the public has grown to expect the library to be the place of first resort to look for the answers to questions.

This suggests questions for further discussion:

- Does this change in usage provide an economic argument for increased funding?
- How do economic principles apply to electronic information services?
- Has the source or amount of support for libraries as a percentage of municipal budgets changed?
- Has the role of state and local government compared to the federal government changed?

10

User Fees I:
The Economic Argument

It started in California, where such maladies are expected, and spread. By the November elections, it had become a nationwide epidemic with cases reported in at least sixteen states. Fatalities were common as familiar public figures passed from the political scene. Proposition 13 fever it was called by some. Others dubbed it a taxpayers' revolt.

Whatever the name, it left in its wake a decline in revenues available to public institutions. Faced with a financial shortfall of shattering proportions, local officials began groping for alternative ways to finance municipal services. One of the most frequently recurring suggestions has been the imposition of user fees.

While most librarians react with moral outrage to the suggestion that user fees be levied, the economic argument for such a course of action is persuasive. This article will outline the basic principles of economics and municipal finance which are considered in such discussions. A subsequent article, in the January 15 issue of *LJ*, will examine the social and political side of the question and some options available to librarians.

Almost one hundred years ago James Bryce, writing in the *American Commonwealth*, suggested two criteria for measuring the effectiveness of government: "What does it pro-

vide for the people and what does it cost the people?" This set of criteria was recently reaffirmed by respondents in a national poll conducted in September 1978 by the *Washington Post*. In all, seven of every eight persons polled reported that they are more concerned with the quality of services received from government than they are with the amount of taxes they pay. Thus, an analysis of the current situation requires an examination of local government expenditures as well as sources of revenue.

Local Expenditures

By any measure, local government expenditure has risen rapidly over recent years. In the period from 1950 to 1975, local expenditure has risen from $17 billion to $162 billion. As a percentage of gross national product, the shift is even more dramatic with state and local government spending increasing from 9.7 percent of the gross national product in 1950 to 17.5 percent in 1975, or an increase of 80 percent, while spending at the federal level grew from 14.8 percent in 1950 to 19.2 percent in 1975, an increase of 30 percent (see table 1). These figures indicate a real quantitative and qualitative growth in the provision of goods and services at the state and local level and a changing role for local government.

Local governments spend money on goods and services which presumably benefit the

TABLE 1
Government Expenditures and Gross National Product

| Year | Gross National Product | Government expenditures* | | | | | |
| | | Amount | | | As a percentage of gross national product | | |
		Total (Billions)	Federal	State and Local	Total	Federal	State and Local
1940	$ 99.7	$ 20.4	$ 9.2	$ 11.2	20.4	9.2	11.2
1950	286.2	70.3	42.4	27.9	24.5	14.8	9.7
1960	506.0	151.3	90.3	61.0	29.8	17.8	12.0
1970	982.4	333.0	184.9	148.1	33.8	18.8	15.0
1975	1,516.3	556.3	291.1	265.2	36.7	19.2	17.5

*Expenditures allocated by final dispersing agency
SOURCE: Department of Commerce, Bureau of the Census

residents of local jurisdictions. Indeed, as we have seen, unless local residents secure some tangible benefits, they cannot be expected either to pay taxes or to reelect public officials who levy the taxes.

In terms of economic theory, there are several reasons why individuals choose to "purchase" certain goods and services through local governments rather than from some other source. These reasons attempt to explain why goods such as education, police and fire protection, and mass transportation are provided by local governments while food, clothing, and most housing are not.

The first advantage to public provision of these goods and services is usually described under the term "efficiency." Political or governmental institutions provide a device that permits individuals to act jointly, thereby securing more goods and services for a given expenditure than each could obtain by acting privately or independently.

In itself, however, efficiency is insufficient to explain public intervention into the market since individuals can and in fact sometimes do form themselves into voluntary cooperative groups. Private clubs and food co-ops are examples of this type of activity. In fact, many publicly supported services began in this man-

ner, e.g., subscription fire departments, private schools, and subscription libraries.

In some circumstances, however, voluntary arrangements designed to capture the economic advantages of joint consumption tend to break down. This most commonly occurs when "exclusion" is either costly or impossible to enforce. By "exclusion," economists mean the ability to prevent those who do not contribute from enjoying the goods or services provided. One fairly obvious example is reduction in air pollution. Since no individual can be excluded from enjoying the benefits of clean air, some individuals might find it advantageous not to share the costs if costs were a matter of voluntary contributions. These individuals would thereby enjoy the benefits without contributing to the costs.

Public and Private Goods

The economic definition of public goods contains these two essential characteristics: relative efficiency in joint consumption and relative inefficiency in exclusion. In the case of a pure public good, the benefits are considered to accrue to society as a whole. National defense is a commonly used example.

At the other extreme are private goods: they can be provided in divisible units; their benefits are not interrelated; and individuals can be excluded from benefits without unduly increasing the costs. When the provision of these goods contains a collective interest (often modest, sometimes obscure), the government may intervene. Examples of private goods provided by public agencies include postal service, parking facilities, and in some states liquor store products.

Most governmental services are found between these extremes, with education and public welfare accounting for more than half of local general expenditures (table 2). An overriding element of these services is their spillover effect, or the degree to which they are beneficial to society as a whole. While education is directly beneficial to individuals, the spillover of benefits is of such social importance that the cost of primary and secondary education is supported by general tax revenues. Public welfare services are another constellation of functions whose benefits accrue to individuals but benefit society collectively because of the value placed on maintenance of some minimal standard of living.

Clearly, spillover effects (also called externalities) occupy a shady area from an economic point of view. By definition, externalities are costs or benefits which cannot be attached to individuals and are frequently difficult to quantify. At the same time, external economies and diseconomies affect not only the quality of life in urban areas, but also the range of functions of the local government. It is here that economics most closely approaches a consideration of social value and attempts to assign some dollar value to polluted air, congested highways, and improved educational attainment.

Local Revenues

In order to provide goods and services it is obviously necessary for government to generate revenue. Municipal revenue is derived from general revenue sources, including tax revenue and nontax revenue, and from nongeneral sources such as utility, liquor store, and insurance trust revenue.

To fully appreciate municipal revenue structures and attendant problems (especially those exacerbated by Proposition 13 and its offspring), it is necessary to briefly review the theory of taxation. Taxes serve three primary functions: generating revenues for the financing of government goods and services; redistributing income; and reducing private income and private spending. This last purpose is basically a fiscal policy function and as such remains a federal responsibility; therefore, it will be excluded from the present discussion.

Some economists contend that income redistribution, too, should be left in the hands of the federal government and removed from discussions of municipal finance. In view of the fact that forms of taxation rest on principles of equity as well as efficiency and result in income redistribution in effect if not in intent, it would appear reasonable to accept income redistribution as a valid consideration in local taxation.

Tax equity is concerned with fairness. Without becoming too technical, there are two principles of tax equity that impinge directly on discussions of user fees and need to be identified: the "ability-to-pay" principle and the "benefit received" principle.

The ability-to-pay principle states that taxes should be distributed among taxpayers according to their financial capacities. In economic language taxes may be regressive, proportional, or progressive. A regressive tax means that the ratio of tax to income declines as income rises. Property tax is generally considered a regressive tax. A proportional tax means the ratio stays the same. A progressive tax means the ratio rises as income rises. A graduated income tax is progressive in theory, although its application under current tax legislation suggests some perversion of the original intent.

The benefit received principle represents an attempt to distribute tax burdens among those enjoying goods or services. Under this

TABLE 2
Local Direct Expenditures for Own Functions (millions)

Year	Total	General								Utility	Liquor Stores	Insurance Trust
		Total	Educa-tion	High-ways	Public Welfare	Health and Hosps.	Police and Fire	General Control	Other			
1940	$ 7,685	$ 6,499	$ 2,263	$ 780	$ 629	$ 309	$ 566	$ 410	$ 1,542	$ 1,090	$ 10	$ 86
1950	17,041	14,754	5,819	1,745	1,374	801	1,179	724	3,112	2,005	80	202
1960	38,847	34,092	15,323	3,358	2,183	1,898	2,607	1,459	7,264	4,066	115	570
1970	91,889	82,582	38,938	5,384	6,477	4,880	5,830	2,961	18,113	7,820	223	1,263
1975	161,042	143,148	64,956	8,270	9,733	9,878	10,528	5,435	34,348	15,276	290	2,327

Percentage Distribution of Expenditures

Year		Total	Educa-tion	High-ways	Public Welfare	Health and Hosps.	Police and Fire	General Control	Other
1940		100	34.8	12.0	9.7	4.8	8.7	6.3	23.7
1950		100	39.4	11.8	9.3	5.4	8.0	4.9	21.0
1960		100	44.9	9.8	6.4	5.6	7.6	4.3	21.3
1970		100	47.2	6.5	7.8	5.9	7.0	3.6	21.9
1975		100	45.4	5.8	6.8	6.9	7.3	3.8	24.0

SOURCE: Department of Commerce, Bureau of the Census; percentage computations by author

principle, taxes are seen as "prices" and distributed at a "cost" equal to the marginal benefit received. This principle is appealing to economists because it relates to both the revenue and expenditure sides of public finance and provides a pleasing symmetry between supply and demand. Beleaguered municipal officials see it as a guide to allocation of resources, since it presumably forces individuals to reveal their preferences for services through willingness to pay. Obviously, this is a pivotal concept in the user fee discussion.

Tax efficiency, as one might guess, refers to the costs of tax collection. An efficient tax is one which imposes minimal costs to the taxpayer in the payment of the tax, and which can be collected and enforced with minimal cost to the taxing unit.

Local government revenues have grown substantially over recent years (table 3), up from $37 million in 1960 to $90 million in 1970 and $160 million in 1975. However, the growth in tax revenues as a percentage has declined and now represents only 38 percent of the total as compared to 48 percent in 1960 and 44 percent in 1970. The relative drop in tax revenue has been made up by a corresponding growth in revenues provided by user charges (23.6 percent in 1975) and intergovernmental transfers (38.8 percent in 1975).

Cities have traditionally relied heavily on property tax. Although this tax has declined significantly in importance in total general revenues, the property tax continues to provide 82 percent of local government's own tax revenues. The impact of the recent attack on property tax as a source of local income cannot be underestimated. Trends toward new tax sources such as city sales and income tax and increased reliance on nontax revenue sources such as user fees and intergovernmental transfers are almost certain to continue at an accelerated rate.

In light of these long-term trends and recent developments, an increased reliance on resource allocation along the lines of the benefit received principle is likely.

User Charges

The use of fees is not a new concept. Charges have traditionally been used to finance bridges and highways, to support hospital and health services, and to pay for public utilities. While current interest in fees has been heightened by the practical need to generate additional revenue to support public services, there does exist a theoretical justification for such a move.

Briefly the argument revolves around: (1) the character of public goods and services; (2) the issue of allocative efficiency; (3) the concept of equity; and (4) developments in the areas of marginal cost pricing. The first of these is basically an examination of those goods and services for which user fees can, practically speaking, be charged. The second and third explore the question of whether user fees should be imposed. The final issue is concerned with how charges should be levied.

As described earlier, public goods are indivisible and potential users are difficult to exclude. It was also noted that many goods and services provided by local governments are not pure public goods, but are in fact divisible, excludable, and are therefore chargeable. The observation that municipal services might better be described in economic terms as private goods with public benefits is not in itself a justification for the use of fees. It does, however, establish the fact that public pricing is possible.

Allocative efficiency flows from the benefit received principle. Economic efficiency is defined as supplying goods and services preferred by the community. The imposition of fees provides a mechanism for determining preference through willingness to pay. Those who favor fees maintain that use of prices helps allocate scarce resources according to the intensity of demand and helps provide a rationale for new investment decisions.

Equity, as noted earlier, is a concept concerned with fairness. It too derives from the benefit received principle and rests on the be-

TABLE 3
Total Local Revenue by Source and Percentage Distribution
Selected Fiscal Years 1902–1975

					From Own Sources								Intergovernmental	
			General Revenue											
				Taxes										
Year	Total[a]	Total own sources	Total general	Total	Property	Sales and gross receipts	Income[b]	License and other	Charges and miscellaneous	Utility	Liquor stores	Insurance trust[c]	From states	From federal[d]
						Amount (Millions)								
1940	7,724	5,792	5,007	4,497	4,170	130	18	179	510	704	13	68	1,654	278
1950	16,101	11,673	9,586	7,984	7,042	484	64	394	1,602	1,808	94	185	4,217	211
1960	37,324	27,209	22,912	18,081	15,798	1,339	254	692	4,831	3,613	136	549	9,522	592
1970	89,082	59,557	51,392	38,833	32,963	3,068	1,630	1,173	12,558	6,608	258	1,299	26,920	2,605
1975	159,731	97,757	84,357	61,310	50,040	6,468	2,635	2,166	23,047	10,867	338	2,194	51,068	10,906
					Percentage Distribution of Revenue from Own Sources[e]									
1940		100.0	86.4	77.6	72.0	2.2	.3	3.1	8.8	12.2	.2	1.2	21.4	3.6
1950		100.0	82.1	68.4	60.3	4.1	.5	3.4	13.7	15.5	.8	1.6	26.2	1.3
1960		100.0	84.2	66.5	58.1	4.9	.9	2.5	17.8	13.3	.5	2.0	25.5	1.6
1970		100.0	86.3	65.2	55.4	5.2	2.7	2.0	21.1	11.1	.4	2.2	30.2	2.9
1975		100.0	86.3	62.7	51.2	6.6	2.7	2.2	23.6	11.1	.3	2.2	32.0	6.8

[a] Duplicative transactions between levels of government are excluded in arriving at aggregates
[b] Principally individual income
[c] Includes collections for unemployment compensation and employee retirement funds
[d] Amounts received directly from federal government, not transfers of federal funds received initially by states
[e] Intergovernmental revenue is shown as a percent of total revenue

SOURCE: Department of Commerce, Bureau of the Census; percentage computations by Tax Foundation

lief that in cases where individual benefits are paramount, the individuals receiving the benefits should bear the costs. While it is not always easy to determine where personal utility stops and social utility starts (as in the case of postsecondary education), other services are more clear-cut (recreation facilities, parking facilities, selected health services). One of the perversions of tax support of some public institutions is a redistribution of effective income from lower to higher income groups. Some authorities argue, for instance, that institutions like community colleges that are used primarily by middle-class students yet supported by all might make higher education available more equitably by charging close to full cost while providing generous financial assistance to those needing it.

The argument for marginal cost pricing of some governmental goods and services rests on complex theories of welfare economics and monopolistic pricing. To abbreviate the discussion, these theories maintain that once a capital-intensive facility operating over a range of decreasing costs is installed, the general welfare goal should be to maximize the use of the facility. Economic efficiency is attained when there is no unsatisfied demand and when price equals marginal cost. Marginal cost is defined as the incremental cost of another unit of output. In a declining cost industry, the marginal cost may be less than the average unit cost, resulting in a deficit. Here the goal of economic efficiency conflicts with the goal of financial sufficiency. The degree to which a community is willing to subsidize a declining cost facility will depend on its importance to the community. It will also depend on the extent to which the community is able to support the activity from general tax revenues.

Questions about the distributional aspects of public pricing are frequently raised in discussions of user fees. The fact that individuals who do not pay would thereby be excluded from using a service forces a reconsideration of social goals and a reexamination of alternatives for meeting these goals. Resources are limited; some mechanism for their allocation is unavoidable.

Historically, in the interest of greater equity, general taxation replaced fees as a method of financing many public services. The poor, it was felt, should have equal access to education. That was fair. But fairness is a slippery term and its application needs to be examined. It is necessary to ask who pays, who benefits, and what the values are of those benefits.

Some services, such as outdoor recreation facilities, are used primarily by middle-income groups although they are supported from general tax revenues. Thus lower income groups are paying taxes to support services they don't want and can't use. Would public pricing be more or less equitable?

Some economists maintain that equity would best be served by the use of public pricing accompanied by income subsidy. Briefly the theory holds that individuals should be guaranteed an income floor and permitted to make their own decisions about services they wish to purchase. While it is not the intent of this article to digress into another economic treatise, it is important to recognize that equity is a principle that requires careful examination to distinguish the apparent from the real. Public pricing in itself should not be seen as a first step toward either the dismantling of our public institutions or the disenfranchisement of our poor.

The Outlook

The immediate outlook for local governments is bleak. Rapidly rising costs of municipal services are likely to continue, exacerbated by the familiar problems of inflation, shortages, and national and international economic uncertainty. At the same time, demands for adequate local government goods and services are likely to remain unabated.

Revenue sources are under attack. Reductions in property tax revenue will initially reduce the capacity of local governments to provide familiar services in the same way. While long-term solutions may be found in increased sales and income tax and stepped-up revenue sharing programs and other intergovernmental transfers (especially from states which have a broader taxing capability), short-term solutions will be sought in diminished services and increased use of public pricing.

The preceding discussion is not an apology for public pricing. It is, instead, an attempt to outline the broader issues confronting municipal officials, issues to which municipal libraries must respond. Library examples have been deliberately omitted in order that the economic argument could be developed in as unbiased and emotion-free manner as possible. The second article, to be published in LJ's January 15 issue, will analyze the role of public libraries and some possible responses to this admittedly difficult situation.

SUGGESTED READINGS

Aronson, J. Richard, and Eli Schwartz, eds. *Management Policies in Local Government Finance.* Washington, D.C.: International City Management Association, 1975.

Maxwell, James A., and J. Richard Aronson. *Financing State and Local Governments.* Washington, D.C.: Brookings Institute, 1977.

Musgrave, Richard A., ed. *Broad-Based Taxes: New Options and Sources.* Baltimore: Johns Hopkins Univ. Pr., 1973.

Mushkin, Selma, ed. *Public Prices for Public Products.* Washington, D.C.: The Urban Institute, 1972.

11

User Fees II:
The Library Response

They [the Americans] have all a lively faith in the perfectibility of man, they judge that the diffusion of knowledge must necessarily be advantageous, and the consequences of ignorance fatal; they all consider society as a body in a state of improvement, humanity as a changing scene, in which nothing is, or ought to be, permanent; and they admit that what appears to them today to be good may be superseded by something better tomorrow.

—Alexis de Tocqueville, *Democracy in America*

Americans love their libraries. In spite of the fact that as institutions, public libraries are poorly used and inadequately supported, the public clings to the notion that libraries are an intrinsic part of a civilized society. The reasons for this phenomenon, which has been demonstrated repeatedly in libraries from New Jersey to California, are not obscure. Libraries rest solidly on assumptions that are fundamental to a democracy: a belief in the perfectibility of man and the preeminence of the democratic form of government.

While a restatement of the library creed may seem extraneous to a discussion of user fees, it is in fact central to the analysis. "User Fees 1: The Economic Argument" (*LJ*, January 1, p. 19–23) briefly outlined the principles of economics and municipal finance which are necessary to a discussion of public pricing.

This second article will deal quite specifically with libraries as they exist within this context. It will examine the social and political justification for libraries, their current use, and possible options.

Librarians have always defined their mission in heroic terms and proclaimed it with an almost religious fervor: ". . . it is of paramount importance that the means of general information should be so diffused that the largest possible number of persons should be induced to read and understand questions going down to the very foundations of social order."[1] "Libraries are now conducted for the many, not for the few. It is our aim to provide something for everyone who can read."[2] "The objectives of the public library . . . in essence are two—to promote enlightened citizenship and to enrich personal life."[3] "The library is the best training ground for enlightenment that rational man has ever conceived."[4] "From an institution with rather general educational, cultural and recreational aims . . . the library will increasingly become a part of our essential machinery for dealing with these concerns."[5]

The library creed, repeated over more than a century, is clear: democracy is desirable; it depends on an educated populace; libraries provide the means for educating members of society to pursue both personal and social goals. Translated into more functional terms, the public library provides the means necessary for the educational, informational, and recreational development of the individual. At the same time it makes available information necessary for a citizen to participate in an informed way in the political process.

The question, of course, is why, if libraries are essential to a democratic society, are they so unsuccessful in attracting support? In economic terms, why are so few resources allocated to the support of public libraries?

The Information Society

Daniel Bell has used the term "post-industrial" to describe contemporary society. It is characterized by the growth and centrality of theoretical knowledge and the expansion of the service sector over a manufacturing economy. It has been estimated that by 1980 some seventy out of every one hundred persons will be engaged in some form of service activity.

Moreover, information occupies an increasingly significant position in a society so heavily involved with service and the creation and transfer of knowledge. In fact, the total revenue of all information industries, including television, radio, postal service, education, research and development, federal information services, and others, amounted to more than $340 billion for 1974. If banking, insurance, and legal services are included as well, the figure climbs to $625 billion. Compared to a gross national product of $1,413.2 billion, information activities account for close to 45 percent of the GNP for that year, and the percentage is growing.[6] It is estimated that by 1980, 55 percent of the entire labor force will be engaged in information occupations.

Public library revenues for 1974 were $1.2 billion or less than .2 percent of the total spent on information.[7] Based on these statistics, it is clear that the position of libraries as primary dispensers of education and information is largely mythical.

People do have information needs, but by and large public libraries are not the institution they choose to fill these needs. In a 1973 study of the *Information Needs of Urban Residents,* it was found that "only three percent of respondents overall used a library to obtain information on their most important problems."[8] A more recent study, using a different population base and asking different but similar questions, revealed that one out of five persons interviewed used the library to obtain information.[9]

Use of public libraries has been repeatedly documented. Between 20 percent and 40 percent of adults use libraries. (Again responses vary depending on the way in which questions are asked and the time period covered.) These library users are predominantly middle and upper-middle class, middle to upper income, white-collar, professional, managerial, better educated individuals. They come to borrow books, read magazines and newspapers, and use reference materials and services.[10]

While some use the library to obtain specific information for personal or professional reasons, most adults use the public library as a source of reading material, and the reading they pursue is primarily recreational.

Public libraries derive the bulk of their revenue, 76 percent, from local sources, with state contributions accounting for 6.6 percent, federal 7.4 percent, and gifts, donations, and fees making up the remaining 10.2 percent.[11] In 1974 expenditures by municipal governments amounted to $140 billion. The library portion, $1.2 billion, was .8 percent of the total, a decline from 1.2 percent of municipal budgets in 1965. In the post-Proposition 13 era with its attack on property tax, which constitutes the major source of municipal revenue, it is unlikely that this trend will be reversed.

Between Scylla and Charybdis

Libraries find themselves today in an uncomfortable position with the Scylla of the information industry on one side and the Charybdis of shrinking municipal revenue on the other. The situation is further exacerbated by the discrepancy between the social justification, which has been the library creed, and the actual use made of libraries, which consists largely of the delivery of recreational reading to the middle class. The introduction of user fees as a source of supplemental funding is seen by many as the beginning of the end of free library service. The unspoken fear persists that library services are essentially valueless to the general public, and that the introduction of charges will result in the death of library service altogether.

In spite of these fears, real or imagined, the economic argument presented in that previous article would appear to have some merit. Surely there is something patently unfair about taxing an entire populace to support a service used by only 20 percent to 40 percent, especially when most of those who do use libraries are economically capable of paying a fee. The benefit received principle suggests that it would be both more equitable and more efficient to install marginal cost pricing and let the services support themselves.

Moreover, library services are not pure public goods in the economic sense. Exclusion is possible and charges can be easily and economically instituted. Although most economists would admit that there are some external benefits to be derived from libraries, measurement of actual use suggests that most benefits accrue primarily to the individuals. There are many institutions which are more successful in educating individuals of every age, and libraries are clearly not the primary source of information needed to maintain a democratic form of government.

What then? To understand the place public libraries hold in contemporary society it is

DEFINITIONS

Public good—A commodity exhibiting two essential characteristics: relative efficiency in joint consumption and relative inefficiency in exclusion.

Externality (spillover)—Uncompensated costs or benefits which occur as a result of some market transaction. Environmental pollution resulting from industrial output is one example of a negative externality.

Benefit received principle—An attempt to distribute tax burdens among those enjoying goods or services.

necessary to separate the rhetoric from the reality and to distinguish what libraries are from what they do. Libraries are political as well as social institutions. As such they fill some deep, inarticulated needs.

Libraries are more than purveyors of information and distributors of books. They are also a symbol of social order. Public libraries embody the cultural, social, political, and economic history of a society. They transmit the ideas, the hopes, the successes and failures of a people. They tell us where we came from and who we are. They are the custodians of value.

This role is one that is assumed by no other institution. It is unprofitable and without immediately measurable results. It is a public good in every sense of the word. The history of a people is indivisible and nonexcludable, although exclusion from access to it is conceivable. It will not, however, attract massive amounts of support.

The Real Dilemma

Public libraries are faced with a dilemma. It is not survival. Libraries will survive even if it is at a reduced level. The question is one of scale and turns back to function. How large will the collection be, what services can libraries provide, and to whom will they provide their services?

Fees and Service

Librarians have several options with respect to user fees. They can become essentially private institutions, install turnstiles at the door, charge admission, and let the market determine their fate. They can cling to ideological purity and resist pricing for any service. They can choose a middle way, maintaining open access and availability while charging for extraordinary and often costly services.

The argument for maintaining libraries as public institutions is compelling. The maintenance of a collective history is a public good. There are external benefits to a society even if they are symbolic. Finally the belief that no one should be excluded from access to knowledge is fundamental to our democratic society. It is not an economic argument, it is a political one.

Should libraries decide to adopt a strict no-fee policy it will undoubtedly be necessary to limit services. A library cannot expand its program while its budget is being cut. Already the trend is apparent. Even stable budgets have lost their purchasing power. In the last five years the average price of a book has increased 53 percent to $18.03 and the average price of a periodical subscription 52 percent to $24.95.[12] The addition of computerized databases and other similar services is probably out of the question for most libraries resolved to resist public pricing.

Many libraries have already chosen a middle course. Services for which fees are already charged include interlibrary loans, reservation of books, fines for overdue books, loans of current best-sellers, film and equipment rentals, and photocopying. Some public libraries even offer specialized reference services for a fee.

It is imperative that librarians clearly distinguish between those activities which are fundamental to the library identity and those services that derive from it. One example familiar to most public librarians is the provision of best-sellers. To what extent should a limited book budget be used to buy multiple copies of currently popular material to satisfy the recreational needs of the middle-class reader? Is that the central role of the public library? Rental collections are a reasonable response. Pricing makes it possible to buy titles in sufficient quantity to satisfy market demand without diminishing resources available for more substantial purchases.

Installation of computerized databases is another area in which public pricing is a sensible solution. These services are used primarily by students and businesses. While there is ample justification for the involvement of libraries in making these services available, serious questions can be raised about supporting them from general tax revenue—especially if such a service results in a reallocation of resources away from other library functions.

Judicious use of public pricing for selected library services is an immediate short-term solution available to library administrators who are faced with major budgetary problems. It permits libraries to preserve their traditional role as custodians of a culture while maintaining services which bring this body of knowledge to the attention of a greater number of people. It is unrealistic to expect that library budgets will miraculously explode into anything approaching adequacy in terms librarians envision in the near future.

Garceau's Prediction

Long-term solutions are to be found in the political arena. While municipal governments will move toward the establishment of new tax bases and increased intergovernmental transfers, public libraries are likely to continue to depend on trying to get a bigger piece of the municipal pie.

In 1949 in his classic treatise on the public library, Oliver Garceau correctly predicted the position of contemporary libraries:

The appeal of the library as an information center seems at first glance to be on more secure political ground. In a world astonished by scientific miracles and in a country where so many values are measured by usefulness, the American library was surely destined to translate its faith into pragmatic terms. The concept that the library shall preserve all important information has therefore been extended to the concept that it shall contain all the information usable in its community. But this brings the library into competition with a political and economic system in which every felt need is served by a government operating and promoting agency or by a profit-seeking commercial enterprise. Such private enterprise, since its life depends upon doing so, will follow closely every wide popular demand. The newspaper, the movies, and the radio proverbially cultivate popular use with great care. The librarian, perhaps, is freer to take an unprofitable risk, but if he inaugurates a service for which the public has a great unmet need, he will in time find his service duplicated and often displaced by a commercial venture. If the public demand is vital and closely connected with other traditional governmental departments, they will take over the means of distributing "practical information." . . . Where the use is general and the need occasional, the library will find that neither private enterprise nor another government agency eager to do the job; but in such cases the public enthusiasm will be correspondingly low.[13]

The fact that libraries are "unprofitable" does not diminish their importance. It is the business of government to support such activities where the benefit to the public is significant. In the case of public libraries, the investment is a small price to pay for a cultural heritage and a symbol of freedom. Without major new political initiatives on the part of librarians, however, financial support is likely to remain about where it is now, a little less than 1 percent of municipal budgets. Expansion and change, if that is desired, will depend in the fi-

nal analysis on the degree to which effective political pressure can be applied at every level.

Use of user fees to finance selected services will lead neither to the salvation of the public library nor to its demise. Public pricing is an economically viable, socially sound way to expand some services and improve others. It should be used, however, only to supplement support from general tax revenue, not to supplant it.

NOTES

1. *Report of the Trustees of the Public Library of the City of Boston,* July 1852. City Document No. 37.

2. Arthur E. Bostwick, "The Future of Library Work," *ALA Bulletin,* 1918, 12:52.

3. Carleton B. Joekel, Amy Winslow, and Lowel Martin, *National Plan for Public Library Service* (Chicago: ALA, 1948), p. 16.

4. President Lyndon B. Johnson on signing the 1964 Library Services and Construction Act.

5. Dan Lacy, "Social Change and the Library: 1945–1980," in Douglas M. Knight and E. Shepley Nourse, *Libraries at Large* (New York: Bowker, 1969).

6. Harvard Program on Information Technologies and Public Policy, *Annual Report, 1976–77, Vol. 1* (Cambridge, Mass.: Harvard, 1977), p. 3.

7. U.S. National Center for Education Statistics, *Survey of Public Libraries, LIBGIS 1,* 1974 (Washington, D.C.: U.S. Department of Health, Education and Welfare, 1977).

8. Edward S. Warner et al., *Information Needs of Urban Residents* (Washington, D.C.: Office of Education, U.S. Department of Health, Education and Welfare, 1973).

9. The Gallup Organization, *The Role of Libraries in America* (Princeton, N.J.: Gallup, 1975).

10. For fuller analysis of library use see: The Gallup Organization, *The Role of Libraries in America* (Princeton, N.J.: Gallup, 1975); Douglas M. Knight and E. Shepley Nourse, eds., *Libraries at Large* (New York: Bowker, 1969); and Angus Campbell and Charles A. Metzner, *Public Use of the Library and Other Sources of Information,* Institute for Social Research (Ann Arbor: Univ. of Michigan, 1950).

11. U.S. National Center for Education Statistics, op. cit.

12. Nada Beth Glick and Sarah L. Prakken, eds., *Bowker Annual of Library and Book Trade Information* (New York: Bowker, 1977).

13. Oliver Garceau, *The Public Library in the Political Process* (New York: Columbia Univ. Pr., 1949).

PART V

The Impact of Technology

L ike politics, technology is very much with us. Indeed, many consider technology to be the major force that is driving libraries rapidly into an ever changing future. The first chapter in this section provides historical perspective. Written in 1991, it preceded the explosion of electronic access that followed the introduction of the World Wide Web and the decision by most libraries to provide Internet access to their users. Reading it again, I am surprised at how accurately we were able to predict the shape of service that we now provide. Some of the issues discussed, such as copyright, are continuing and show no sign of early resolution. Others, such as delivery of full text, have been resolved (at least from a technical perspective) and even eclipsed by today's more pressing challenge of sorting out information available from literally millions of homepages.

Out of this blizzard of information several new and frustrating issues have arisen. "Sex, Kids, and the Public Library" is one take on the political problem of providing unimpeded access to everything on the Web for everyone regardless of age. "Reference Revolutions" takes on the challenge of scholarly publishing as it tries to find the way between the demand for fast, easy access to recent research and the supply that continues to be controlled by a few multinational corporations that persist in extortionate pricing practices. Previously unpublished testimony before the Advisory Committee on Public Interest Obligations of Digital Television Broadcasters is a first cut at yet another new technology.

"The Yin and Yang of Knowing" examines the interaction of print and electronic information and documents and suggests that books continue to have an important place in the minds, hearts, homes, and libraries of the world. It accepts the premise that the first article predicted—easy access to electronic information—and asks what it all means.

This search for meaning in a world with more information than we can ever hope to digest suggests some questions:

- Do we use electronic information differently than print?
- Does this change how we think about books?
- What does this suggest for the future of libraries?
- How can we keep track, keep pace, and look forward to plan for the future of libraries?

Many writers and pundits have recently opined that electronic technology will render books and libraries obsolete and that in the future we will each rely on our own computer, getting every book, article, or piece of data we need electronically. Although I addressed that topic in the "Yin and Yang" article, I wondered what the public in general thought, and in 1998 included a question about library services on a routine public opinion poll. We read a statement and asked those polled to agree, disagree, or have no opinion. The statement was: "Because of the increased use of computers and information technology, libraries are more important than they used to be." Eighty-one percent agreed.

12

Library Automation: The Next Wave

Imagine, if you will, the following scenario. It is past midnight. Unable to sleep, you decide to begin work on a new research project. After fixing yourself a cup of tea, you pad into your home office and fire up your personal computer. Using a modem, you log on to the library's computer system.

First, you check the library's catalog of holdings and place electronic reserves on those monographs you would like to examine. Those items may be picked up at the nearest branch library or delivered to your office the following day. Next, you search the electronic index of periodical literature. You read the abstracts, and determine which articles you would like to read in full. The full text of those items may then be downloaded to your computer, where you will read them at a later date either in electronic format or from printed copy.

Switching to the OCLC Epic Service, you identify additional titles that you will need and arrange electronically for the interlibrary loan of those items. Finally, depending on the nature of your search, you examine specialized databases such as *ERIC, Chemical Abstracts,* or *Engineering Index*. Additional information and citations found in this manner also will be downloaded for review when you are more

Reprinted from *Library Administration & Management*, v. 5, no. 1, 1991

fully awake. Before signing off you remember that you are planning to buy your son a bicycle for his birthday, and you consult the electronic version of *Consumer Reports*. Finally, able to sleep and secure in the knowledge that you have a jump on your research, you return to bed.

This scene is not far-fetched, and it is not far off. Although there may be some variation in the mechanics of how systems will operate, services to be delivered as libraries move beyond bibliography to electronic information and text delivery are pretty straightforward. Academic libraries may deliver information via the wired campus while public libraries provide access through branch libraries and dial-up ports. Still the next wave will be full text and information delivery. Two years ago the Cleveland Public Library adopted a plan to make the scene described above possible within five years. This paper will describe that plan, progress to date, problems that have been encountered, and unanticipated findings.

The Cleveland Plan

The main library of the Cleveland Public Library is the third largest public research collection in the country. It has holdings of nearly eight million items, over two million of which are in book form. It contains 1.6

million titles, over 16,000 current serials titles, and actively collects material in thirty-six languages. In size and scope this collection is comparable to many ARL libraries and surpasses the two ARL libraries in northeastern Ohio. It is, in fact, used extensively by faculty and students in area colleges and universities as well as by area businesses and individuals pursuing independent research projects.

The Cleveland Public Library believes that a public research library has a responsibility to make its resources widely available and remotely accessible. One vehicle for achieving this goal is CLEVNET, an area-wide automated service operated by the Cleveland Public Library. It serves eighteen member libraries covering fifty-four thousand square miles in northeast Ohio. Originally developed as an economical way for libraries to reduce costs and share resources, CLEVNET began by providing automated cataloging, bibliographic control, and circulation services.

The Cleveland Plan for automation development describes growth beyond these traditional services. The plan describes a path by which the Library will offer automated system indexes and bibliographic databases published in electronic format, full-text periodical back-files converted to electronic format, and gateways to external databases. This range of services, including the online catalog, is already accessible locally through approximately six hundred terminals located in libraries throughout the area and available remotely from microcomputer-based workstations using a modem to access the Library's computer. It also includes the electronic delivery of information via telefacsimile where appropriate.

Specifically, the Cleveland Plan sets the following public service goals by year:

1988

Provide remote public access to the online catalog.

1989

Establish a local area network (LAN) in Main Library.

Increase online storage capacity of central site equipment.

Implement online interface with major jobber using acquisition software.

1990

Provide network access to indexes and databases published on CD-ROM.

Replace some public access terminals with multipurpose workstations.

1991

Convert periodical holdings to electronic format.

Provide remote public access to network services.

Progress to Date

Surprisingly, Cleveland Public Library is on schedule in the achievement of this ambitious program. Not surprisingly, we have often taken the great circle route to get from where we are to where we wanted to be. Goals have remained constant, even as means for achieving those goals have shifted and changed.

The first goal was to provide remote public access to the online catalog. The purpose of this was to make it possible for individuals in their home, dormitory, or office to have dial-up access to the holdings of the Cleveland Public Library, the CLEVNET libraries, and the Union List of Periodicals available in fifty-six libraries of all types in the Cleveland metropolitan area. The obvious benefits were an extension of the hours of library service, the promotion of the use of library resources throughout the greater Cleveland area, and the development of a platform for later expansion of remote access to information services. We were concerned about the number of ports that would be needed to support dial-up access, the ability of delivery systems to get material out quickly, and the ever present problem of "hackers" who might try to break into the system and alter significant elements.

The overnight reaction to the availability of the service surpassed our expectations.

Within the first week we increased the number of ports available from eight to sixteen. We found that delivery systems that previously had been established between public, academic, and special libraries in the Cleveland area were adequate to support increased requests for materials. And, yes, there were "hackers" who tried to break into the system, but so far the eternal vigilance of our computer staff has paid off.

In 1989, we did establish a local area network (LAN) in the Main Library. A fiber-optic backbone was installed between the two buildings that comprise the Main Library complex. Additional cabling and network equipment were installed to support departmental microcomputers in all Main Library departments. Although not as glamorous as dial-up access, this step was essential to improving overall system performance. It also allowed the integration of microcomputers as multipurpose departmental workstations. This step was necessary to provide a platform for adding services locally and providing more sophisticated gateways to external databases.

In much the same vein, in 1989 the Library increased the online storage capacity of central site equipment and implemented an online interface with major jobbers using acquisitions software. In 1990 the Library will begin to provide network access to indexes and selected databases. This goal is being achieved, however, in a far different manner than initially envisioned. When the Cleveland Plan was originally developed we imagined the use of items on CD-ROMs that would be housed in jukeboxes and networked electronically. Instead, we have established a relationship with Information Access Corporation (IAC) to provide electronic access to indexing of the current three years of 1,200 journal titles. As this article is being written, this service is scheduled to come online in two weeks; its impact is unknown. The Cleveland Public Library also is investigating the possibility of making OCLC's Epic database available on a dial-up basis.

In 1990 Cleveland Public Library is beginning to experiment with the provision of gateway access to other databases. Cleveland FREENET, which provides community bulletin board service and is itself a gateway to academic libraries in Ohio and California, already is accessible through the Library's automated system, and the Cleveland Public Library is on the Internet as well.

The most ambitious goal for 1991, and possibly for the entire automation effort, is the conversion of periodicals from paper to electronic storage. The Cleveland Public Library currently has over twelve linear miles of bound periodicals in a building that is rapidly running out of space. Like other research libraries, we are looking for ways to reduce our space requirements while we increase accessibility to information. Already the Library has replaced as much of its periodical collection as possible with commercially available microforms, but microforms only solve space problems and do not yet contribute to increased accessibility. Ultimately, conversion of periodical materials to optical disc storage will help solve both storage and accessibility problems. Unfortunately, the costs for any single library to convert these older materials is prohibitive. Moreover, such a move raises important copyright issues.

Legal Issues

It is no surprise that legal issues present the knottiest set of problems that confront libraries interested in extending accessibility and use via computer and communication technologies. The meaning of copyright in the "post-paper age" is yet to be resolved. Interpretations abound concerning the meaning of a preservation copy in this environment. If a library converts a document covered by copyright to optical disc storage to preserve that item from disintegration, one might argue that the library is not in violation of copyright laws. If, in response to an interlibrary loan request, that same library makes a copy of a document for use by a researcher, one might assume that is fair use. But if that same library provides a means of electronic interlibrary loan, whereby the requesting library or individual could access the material directly, without the physical intervention of a library staff member, publishers would argue that that is a violation of copyright.

The purpose of this article is not to argue for one interpretation or another of the copyright laws. Rather, it suggests that the solution is most likely to be found through cooperation and experimentation. Publishers are concerned about protecting the revenue stream that supports their business. Libraries are concerned with increasing the accessibility of information in an economical fashion while decreasing the amount of the library budget dedicated to stratospherically priced scholarly journals. These goals are not necessarily mutually exclusive. It is possible that new pricing mechanisms can be developed that will both protect publishers and expand library services. These pricing mechanisms rest on the assumptions that production costs can be reduced and that use can be expanded. At present the situation is analogous to two children standing outside a dark room fearful of monsters that may be in the room. To allay the fear of imagined monsters, it is necessary to walk in and turn on the light. The purpose of an experiment like the one going on between the Cleveland Public Library and Information Access Corporation is to provide measurable information about the impact of electronic services.

Closely related to legal issues are pricing issues. The pricing issue coin has two sides. On the one side we find pricing mechanisms by which libraries pay publishers. On the other, we encounter fees libraries charge users. Traditionally, electronic publishers have relied on connect time as the basic pricing mechanism. Libraries are reluctant to make such services available to end-users directly because they represent a potential blank check. In order to mediate and control costs, libraries conventionally require that searches be done by library staff. If direct searching by end-users could become a controllable cost, it might be possible to reduce staff costs involved in each transaction.

From the library point of view, the simplest approach to solving this problem is for the library to pay a licensing fee. Licensing fees are easier to negotiate for academic libraries with a measurable and identifiable base of users than they are for public libraries. Understandably, publishers fear that if just anyone can dial up the public library and have access to the database, other libraries will cancel their subscriptions. While many librarians do not feel that this would be the result, their assurances are unconvincing to publishers and we find ourselves back at the door of the dark room.

The issue of fee-based services is a larger one for public libraries than it is for academic libraries. It is wrong, the argument goes, for a public library to limit access to information in any way, especially by fees. Nevertheless, public libraries have always charged fees for some services and that practice is likely to continue. One of the services most libraries charge fees for is the copying of documents.

The Cleveland Public Library manages to stay in the middle of this debate by providing free access to materials that individuals wish to copy for themselves (except, of course, for the cost of the copying machine itself) while charging a copying fee to those individuals who would like to save the price of parking and have us mail or fax an item out. Copying fees will continue to be necessary whether the copying is done by a real person or through the electronic downloading of full text. In addition, as we move into electronic document delivery we expect a copyright fee to be a part of the cost. The remainder of the charge will be dedicated to maintaining the system that makes remote access possible.

A final issue that should be mentioned is the ultimate impact of electronic publishing and delivery of scholarly journals on scholarly publishing. Presently, once an article is published, there is no way to measure its readership. If it were possible (and it will be possible) to measure readership, one might assume some impact on questions of academic promotion and tenure.

Surprises

When the Cleveland Public Library began its expansion of automated services, we expected that remote use of materials would replace in-house use of materials. Instead quite the opposite has occurred. In the two years since the Library's catalog became available on dial-up access, circulation has increased 34 percent, reference service has increased 115 percent, interlibrary loan has increased 86 percent, and most surprising of all, walk-in use of the Library has increased 25 percent. The overall impact is quite simply that more people are using more materials in more ways. The situation is analogous to that faced by banks when bank teller machines were installed to replace human tellers. Instead, what the banks found, and what libraries are finding now, is that transactions have simply increased.

CPL staff find that individuals frequently conduct electronic searches at home and come into the library with printouts from their computers in spite of the fact that those items could have been sent out to them. Patrons indicate that in their search they found so much more material than they expected that it became necessary to visit the library to sort through it all. In the simplest terms, dial-up access to the Library's catalog is our best advertisement. People are continually surprised at the size and scope of the collection and delighted to discover that we have just what they need.

The Cleveland Plan is one ripple in the new wave of automated services. Technology has made it possible for libraries to move decisively beyond bibliography to serve scholars, students, businesses, and just plain folks. There is much to be done, many issues to be resolved, and much to learn about the impact of our new services. Full-text delivery is not the last wave, but it is the next wave.

13

Sex, Kids, and the Public Library

"Sex at the library. News at eleven." Television, talk shows, and newspapers are shouting the message in community after community across the country from Orange County to Boston, from Oklahoma City to Medina, from Houston to New York. They say that public libraries are no longer safe havens for children. They say that ALA has libraries peddling pornography. They say that librarians are unresponsive to the public's concern. They say that something must be done.

The problem is a knotty one. How does a library provide free and open access to the thirty-four million sites now available worldwide through the Internet without inflaming parents and others in the community concerned about their children viewing pictures that most believe are pornographic? It is one thing to fight the Communications Decency Act in court for its obvious legal failings and quite another to confront a room full of enraged parents and elected officials armed with pictures printed from the Internet in a public library.

This article is not meant to deal with the legal aspects of pornography on the Internet. I believe that the current position of the American Library Association in its suit challenging the Communications Decency Act is appropriate. What I fear, however, is that we may win in court and lose in the court of public

Reprinted from *American Libraries,* June/July 1997

opinion. The very real issues arising from pornography on the Internet are not going to be resolved by the courts. They are going to be resolved by public libraries and public library users. How they are resolved will determine whether public libraries continue to be the most respected (maybe the only respected) public institution in the country.

In spite of the official ALA position outlined in the *Library Bill of Rights* that there should be free and open access to all library materials for everyone regardless of age, including material on the Internet, libraries across the country are experimenting with some mechanism for limiting child access at least to the seamier sites. Some are using the technological solution of filtering software; others have sought legal sanction by requiring parental approval for children to use the Internet; still others rely on behavioral responses such as making the computer screen public, making the computer screen private, or asking users to desist when viewing offensive images.

The problem with all of the solutions currently available is that none of them work and many of them are creating additional, unanticipated problems. Current filtering software screens out some material we want left in and leaves in material we want screened out; it suggests to the public that the problem is solved when it is not. It doesn't take a child without parental approval long to borrow someone else's card. Monitoring screens may put library staff in an awkward position. Whatever the official position of ALA on this subject, there is no question in my mind that were filtering software available that reliably filtered out the "adults only" sites without screening out information on sexually transmitted diseases and breast cancer, libraries would leap at the chance to install it.

In the absence of a technological silver bullet, we are struggling to solve a radically new problem with old paradigms. With the Internet we are now offering the public material we have not, and in some instances would not, select. What does censorship mean in this context? What is our real responsibility to children? What is the purpose of the public library from the public's point of view?

Intellectual freedom is a bedrock issue for libraries. Most of us at one time or another have been called upon to defend a selection decision and are proud of our ability to defend the retention of Judy Blume, J. D. Salinger, or Salman Rushdie. Some of us make and defend more controversial purchases like Madonna's *Sex*. Most libraries make these decisions and defend them on the basis of a well-thought-out, carefully crafted selection policy. Our selection policies and the library profession's strong defense of intellectual freedom are grounded in our conviction that libraries serve individuals rather than groups, and our communities have a wide spectrum of social, political, and religious belief. Moreover, access to a broad spectrum of ideas is fundamental to a democracy.

Nevertheless, there has always been material that most libraries don't buy. (Much of what can be found in an adult bookstore falls into this category.) When we make these judgments we call it selection. When we choose to exclude material we call it censorship. Evidence suggests that the distinction lacks meaning in an electronic environment. Consider the following: Public Library A decides to handle the furor over a child's access to pornographic material by selecting several hundred sites out of the thirty-four million

available as appropriate to children and making those, and only those, available in its children's room. Public Library B decides to install filtering software that blocks access to several thousand questionable sites. Which library is providing better access to more information? The one that selects or the one that censors? Is it any less valid to "select out" material than it is to "select in" material?

Many have argued that selection is cost driven, that no library can afford to buy everything and selection policies codify priorities. Many claim that there is no marginal cost involved in providing access to everything on the Internet because once a library is wired there is no separate charge for each site accessed. Yet consider the following: a representative of one large urban library that has recently installed banks of computers privately acknowledges that at any given time as many as half of the PCs available are being used to view pornography. Is this the library's purpose in installing the computer system? Can we say that access is free? What about costs for hardware, software, and space? The cost for the material itself is only a small part of total costs.

Purists argue that if we "select out" some material we are opening the door for would-be censors to impose even greater constraints on our collections. This argument sounds very much like the "domino theory," a diplomatic posture that has become obsolete in our post-cold-war era. In truth there is some feeling that by casting our protective net wide enough to cover material that would be illegal in many communities we are losing our credibility in defending other selection decisions.

The issues here are far from being resolved. The ACLU is threatening to sue libraries for use of blocking software, for asking library users to remove offending images from screens, for failure to provide private viewing places, for almost anything that doesn't ensure full access to everything by everyone. Some library users have asked out loud if public viewing of pornography constitutes a new form of sexual harassment. Some political jurisdictions are tying library funding to the use of filtering software, while others have discussed imposing fines on anyone providing children access to pornography. (Most libraries are currently exempt from such laws.)

At the heart of this debate is nothing less than the definition of the role of the public library. We must never forget that public libraries belong to the public. We hold them in trust for present and future generations and ultimately public libraries will be what the public wants them to be. If we want the community to hear and understand our position on these issues we must hear and understand theirs. We must search together for a solution that will enable parents to continue to send their children to the public library with confidence without eroding our ability to meet the information needs of adults with vastly different opinions and orientations.

Within the profession we must treat each other with respect as well and avoid saying, as one prominent ALA representative said to a librarian in a public meeting in Ohio last year, that the librarian should "look for another career" because he dared to disagree with her position on this topic. We need the best thinking of everyone, even, maybe especially, those who are not repeating conventional wisdom.

What is censorship in this environment? Censorship is what happens if we are forced to pull the plug on the Internet because legal or financial constraints make it impossible for us to do anything else. Censorship occurs if we deprive citizens who are unable to afford computers access to a world of information now found on the thirty-four million Web sites (a number that is doubling every three months), thereby effectively redlining people because of their economic condition. Censorship is providing nothing to anyone because we are unwilling or unable to search for new solutions appropriate to an electronic age.

14

Reference Revolutions

Last year at a Summit of World Library Leaders held by the New York Public Library, fifty representatives of some of the largest libraries in the world met to discuss global library strategies for the twenty-first century. As one might expect, talk quickly turned to the challenges and opportunities provided by rapidly changing electronic technologies. In the course of the meeting one of the participants described the struggle of his library to help users gain better access to the now more than thirty-six million Web sites available worldwide (a number that is said to double every three months). He described the problem of getting hundreds, sometimes thousands, of "hits" when an individual tries to do even a simple search and talked about the need for libraries to apply knowledge classification schemes to electronic information. After he spoke, other members of the group reported dealing with the same problem and talked about their attempts to identify and classify databases that are especially helpful. Each of us, it seemed, was struggling with the same problem, and each library was duplicating the efforts of every other. It was a familiar problem.

Reprinted from *Journal of Library Administration,* v. 25, no. 2/3, 1998

The OCLC Story

On July 5, 1967, ten leaders of academic institutions in the state of Ohio conspired to revolutionize libraries forever. These ten—three university presidents, three university vice presidents, and four university library directors—met on the campus of Ohio State University to act on a plan proposed by Frederick Gridley Kilgour, one of the library profession's great seminal thinkers. Kilgour had observed that libraries across the nation and around the world were spending millions of dollars doing the same work over and over again. At that time the object of all the duplication was cataloging.

It is hard to remember now that until the last few decades every single library in the world was responsible for cataloging its own material. Even though the Library of Congress printed and sold catalog cards, each library, like every school at Harvard, was a tub on its own bottom. Every time a library received a new book it was responsible for verifying the author and title, assigning subject headings and a classification number, and printing and filing cards with the information in the library's card catalog (a monstrous and often error-ridden remnant of another time that has lately become the object of nostalgia in some quarters). At a cost of $30 to $60 per title, the price of all this duplication was enormous, and libraries saw more and more of their resources going into cataloging with less and less available to buy more titles or provide better reference services.

Kilgour believed that the solution to this duplication was a shared effort that could be facilitated by information storage and retrieval systems that were becoming small enough and fast enough to handle the load. He believed that instead of waiting for the top-down efforts of the Library of Congress, which were often slow and cumbersome, libraries could function as a single unit held together by wires and electronic pulses. He believed that a title could be cataloged once, by a library in Texas or Massachusetts, and that the efforts of that library could then be shared with other libraries. Now we take the system that has become OCLC for granted, but in 1967 it was a revolutionary idea, and the articles of incorporation signed that fateful day in July were for a nonprofit organization called the Ohio College Library Center.

Four years later, on August 26, 1971, the Alden Library at Ohio University cataloged 133 books online and made history as the first library in the world to do online cataloging. Within a year Ohio University increased the number of titles cataloged by one-third while reducing its cataloging staff by seventeen positions. Kilgour's vision, that OCLC would increase access to information while reducing costs, was beginning to be realized.

As remarkable as that first year was, it was just the beginning, and while Ohio University was the first to use this remarkable new service, it was far from the last. By the end of 1980 when Kilgour stepped down as president of OCLC, the number of staff had grown from two to five hundred, the number of participating libraries had grown from the 54 academic libraries in Ohio to 2,300 libraries in all fifty states, and the bibliographic database went from zero to five million. Today the OCLC cataloging system handles over a billion transactions a year, with message traffic running as high as 110 messages a second. Today more than 24,000 libraries in sixty-three countries catalog more than forty million books a year as well as other materials, such as maps, musical scores, and sound recordings. The bibliographic database, now called WorldCat, contains nearly thirty-eight million records and over 660 million location listings. It contains holdings in 377 languages and grows at the rate of two million original records per year. It is the single most consulted database in higher education.

As the database has grown, libraries have found other uses for it that go beyond cataloging. Foremost among them has been resource sharing. This year libraries will borrow over eight million items from each other, using the information and support available through OCLC as an adjunct to WorldCat. This easy availability of often obscure material to anyone, literally anywhere on Earth has revolutionized again the way we think about libraries.

The Reference Story

Fred Kilgour's vision did not stop with cataloging. Shortly after it was clear that shared cataloging was a success, he began talking and writing about moving "beyond bibliography." He believed, and continues to believe, that OCLC can provide not just information about where to find information, but the information itself—the text of the book or article, the map, the recording—each delivered directly to the user. Initially, Kilgour's vision made librarians nervous. Some wondered aloud if OCLC would end up competing with libraries, competing with the very institutions it was established to serve. The debate did not last long as it soon became clear that in providing reference services OCLC was doing exactly what it had done so successfully in providing cataloging: it was enabling libraries to work together to do more than any one of them could do alone. Providing information that could be used directly by library patrons expanded conventional services in a way that strengthened libraries. Once again, OCLC was helping libraries use scare resources cooperatively to provide access to more information for less money.

The OCLC FirstSearch service was introduced in 1991. It was designed to be used by both librarians and library patrons, a departure from the bibliographic databases. Like shared cataloging, FirstSearch started small, although small looked different in 1991 than it did in 1971. Initially six databases were mounted on FirstSearch: WorldCat; ERIC (Educational Resources Information Center); GPO Monthly Catalog; Consumers Index to Product Evaluations; BIOSIS/FS, a database created for FirstSearch that is derived from the Biological Abstracts portion of BIOSIS Previews; and MiniGeoRef, the most recent five years of GeoRef. Initially, FirstSearch was priced by the search, as were other similar databases such as Dialog and Lexis/Nexis.

Today FirstSearch offers access to over sixty-five databases including WorldCat, the *New York Times,* and *World Book Encyclopedia.* It provides bibliographic information, abstracts or articles, and full text. It is distributed through more than 6,200 libraries in forty-four countries including China, Japan, and Australia. The rate of use has climbed to 200,000 searches a day. In a recent issue of a quarterly report called *Information Market Indicators,* Martha Williams reports that First-Search is now the number one online vendor of professional and scholarly databases. Additionally, in response to library requests, OCLC now provides subscription based pricing for FirstSearch, enabling libraries to budget accurately and avoid becoming a victim to the success of the new service. (Many librarians feared that direct user access and success in getting needed information could result in almost unlimited charges with the continuation of a per-use pricing formula.) The availability of FirstSearch over the Internet has further reduced costs by removing incremental communications costs for many libraries in the United States while helping libraries outside the United States overcome international telecommunications barriers.

The most astonishing thing about First-Search is not its progress to date, but the certain knowledge that the reference revolution is still in its infancy. Like the early online cat-

alog now know as WorldCat, growth is geometric, with FirstSearch now growing at the rate of 50 percent a year. If this trend continues, and there is no reason it should not, First-Search itself should account for over one billion searches a year in just seven more years. The reason this rate of growth is likely to continue is that, like WorldCat, FirstSearch provides a mechanism for libraries to do more cooperatively than any one library could do alone, and at a lower cost. In this case the duplication is not in the creation of catalog records, but in the negotiations with electronic producers of information. But there is much more to reference services than providing full text, and in these important developing areas libraries are finding themselves better able to do more by working cooperatively through OCLC than any one library could do on its own.

The Next Chapter

The next stage of development for First-Search will see the introduction of OCLC FirstSearch Electronic Collections Online, Electronic Archiving, and Integrated Searching. In the recent summary of OCLC's strategic plan called *Beyond 2000,* the problem is described succinctly:

"Despite rapid advances in electronic publishing and delivery technology, benefits to libraries and readers of scholarly journals have been slow in coming. Among the key reasons:

- High journal costs, and duplicate print and electronic costs, have been a barrier to progress.
- Archival Services, which are key to avoiding duplicate costs and realizing the economies of the electronic media, have not been forthcoming."

The new three-part initiative described in the strategic plan will be to:

- "Create a cost-effective, Web-based, scaleable delivery system for online journals and rapidly build a collection with a 'critical mass' of journals by topic areas.

- Create a suite of archival services encompassing long-term inexpensive storage, access for both content providers and third parties, scanning, indexing, and technology migration.
- Migrate toward integrated reference solutions embracing FirstSearch, Site-Search, and Electronic Collections Online to realize the vision of seamless access for the information user across a full range of information, including Web resources."

Electronic Collections Online will enable libraries to subscribe to both print and electronic journals from many publishers in a discipline and access them remotely through a single Web interface that will support searching through multiple journals and extensive browsing. Journals that libraries subscribe to will be loaded in their entirety either on or before publication date. In addition to current service OCLC will provide continuing access to the archives of the journals to which they have subscribed. As more journals are issued in electronic form, this service will provide an easy and cost-effective way to manage large electronic collections.

Electronic archiving will go beyond maintaining runs of journal holdings. As more and more materials are digitized, librarians are understandably concerned about document preservation and access into the future. The stability of electronic storage has not yet been demonstrated, and to date changing technology has required continual shifts from one format to another. Many of us as individuals have experienced the loss of data stored on a disc that became so obsolete that no machine could read it any longer. Whole chunks of census data have been lost to the rapid migration of technology. To meet the challenge of preserving electronic documents or documents converted to an electronic format, OCLC is moving toward services that would support long-term, inexpensive storage for libraries individually and collectively. These

services will include access for both content providers and users, scanning, indexing, and technology migration. This cooperative approach to preservation and access is essential if libraries are to move beyond the current level of confidence in their ability to serve patrons in the future.

Integrated Searching will not only allow library users to search numerous FirstSearch databases simultaneously, but it will also allow users to search both print and nonprint material. As any user of the World Wide Web knows, actually finding what you want from the welter of what is available can be a daunting task. Although books and other print documents are typically classified by subject, users of the Web are forced to rely on key word searching, a process that mingles subjects that are unrelated and leaves the searcher with thousands of hits to sort through. Already OCLC has started work on a system (called the Scorpion System) that will explore the possibility of automatically assigning hierarchical subject headings to many of the electronic items now available. This combination of automated retrieval and more conventional organizational structures has the potential for making electronic information more accessible and usable than it is today.

Electronic Publishing—Another Revolution?

Although not yet on the planning horizon, it is not hard to imagine that sometime in the next few years OCLC might enter the publishing arena in a big way. For years researchers have wondered out loud why commercial publishers should get rich by taking information from scholars for free while selling it back to university libraries for what some characterize as extortion prices. Independent electronic publishing has been touted as an alternative to commercial publishing but until recently has been inhibited both by the technical limitation in transmitting charts and other graphic material and the specter of an electronic free-for-all that could result in publication that bypasses the peer review process. With the solution to the problem of capturing and transmitting graphics solved and made easily available on the Web, scientists and scholars are once again wondering what value commercial publishers bring to the distribution of scholarly information. Some are examining ways to keep the current review process without going through commercial publishers.

Commercial publishers are beginning to offer their journals online. Elsevier, for instance, now makes all of its 1,100 titles available electronically. In addition, smaller operations are beginning to make a mark. The Association of Research Libraries reports that the number of electronic journals has grown from fewer than thirty in 1991 to more than three hundred in 1995. Still the problem of pricing remains. The average cost of a scholarly journal has tripled since 1985, forcing research libraries to reduce subscriptions and shift resources away from other materials. Pricing of electronic journals by commercial publishers has not settled down but few expect to see any significant reduction in costs.

HighWire Press, a division of Stanford Libraries, has recently demonstrated what a university working alone can do. Starting in January 1995 with the publication of the *Journal of Biological Chemistry (JBC)*, HighWire is nearly self-supporting, after only two years. More importantly, however, the HighWire effort has demonstrated that quality can be maintained in an electronic environment, without high costs.

OCLC has also been successful in maintaining quality with its publication of *The Online Journal of Current Clinical Trials*, the world's first peer-reviewed online medical journal, which OCLC and the American Association for the Advancement of Science started in July, 1992, and which is now published by Chapman and Hall.

It doesn't take much of a leap to imagine what might happen if OCLC, with its experience in networking, electronic distribution of information, electronic publishing, electronic archiving, and integrated searching, joined forces with universities responsible for the creation of scholarly information. The result would be quicker, easier, cheaper access to scholarship around the world. It would be nothing less than a complete transformation of scholarly publishing. Researchers themselves would continue to write, edit, and provide peer review for scholarly articles. The activity could be organized by scholars themselves through their universities, with universities having particularly strong departments in specific disciplines leading the way. OCLC could provide electronic publication and distribution, using many of the systems already in place. Costs and benefits could be shared in much the same way that costs and benefits are shared through cooperative cataloging. The benefit to the scholar would be more immediate access to the latest research. The benefit to the university and the library would be a reduction in pricing.

Hard to imagine? It's probably no harder to imagine that academic institutions could collaborate to revolutionize the distribution of scholarly research than it was in 1967 for those ten academics in the state of Ohio to imagine that they could transform cataloging and thereby reduce costs. The goals are the same: speed up the flow of information and cut costs. The means are the same: use computer and communications technologies to link individuals and institutions. Even the motivation is the same: reduce wildly escalating costs that are overtaking the ability of libraries to provide a broad base of service. In 1967 it was cataloging costs that limited public service. In thirty years OCLC has made it possible for libraries to reduce the cost to catalog one item from $30 or $60 to less than $2. Today the cost of scholarly journals has ballooned out of control. In the last thirty years, catalog cards have become largely obsolete. Has the time now come for commercial scholarly publishers to become obsolete?

Cooperation among research institutions through OCLC for the independent publication of scholarly material would do more than reduce costs. It would also speed up delivery, eliminate the need for interlibrary loan, eliminate many of the current copyright problems, and enhance scholarship. Universities that were Internet contributors would be rewarded for their contributions, not penalized by the need to buy increasingly expensive journals.

The OCLC Mission

OCLC was founded in 1967 as a membership organization to serve libraries and library users for the following purposes (Beyond 2000: A Summary of OCLC's Strategic Plan, OCLC, 1997):

Maintain and operate a computerized library network.

Promote the evolution of libraries, library use, and librarianship.

Provide services for library users and libraries.

Increase availability of library resources to library patrons.

Reduce library costs.

Further ease of access to and use of the ever-expanding body of worldwide scientific, literary and educational knowledge and information.

Throughout its thirty-year history OCLC has evolved to meet the needs of libraries by using the latest technological capabilities. First it reduced cataloging costs and speeded up the delivery of quality cataloging. Building on that resource, it used the existence of its enormous bibliographic database to encourage resource sharing. OCLC then moved beyond bibliography to provide not just information about information, but the information itself. In the next few years it will add archiving and integrated searching, services that will further encourage the use of electronic information by providing confidence that documents can be found in the short run and preserved for posterity.

Cataloging was just the beginning, a tool to get the information we need. Reference has always been the goal. OCLC reference services are in their infancy. The one thing we can be sure of is that by working cooperatively, using the mechanism libraries have created through OCLC, libraries and their users can look forward to more information faster, at a lower cost, now and tomorrow.

15

Educational Programming in the Digital Era

My purpose is to bring to your attention the ongoing role and responsibility of public libraries in those areas that intersect with the functions and concerns of digital broadcasters.

Public libraries are our most democratic institutions. Their job is to provide every man, woman, and child regardless of age, race, level of education, economic condition, or physical ability or disability with the knowledge and information he or she needs, at the time, place, and in the format needed. Thus, we are democratic in the people, or audience, we serve and in the services, or programming, that we provide.

Because libraries are modestly funded, some of you may be unaware of the range of our reach. A poll that was completed just this week in Cleveland, for instance, revealed that 77 percent of city residents have been in a library in the past year. All of these people are inner-city residents where close to 30 percent are below the poverty level. They include young children and senior citizens, owners of small businesses, students, people struggling to get a job, learning to read, getting information about public assistance, or simply reading the newspaper, or, perhaps, a good book.

Reprinted from testimony by the author before the Advisory Committee on Public Interest Obligations of Digital Television Broadcasters, January 16, 1998.

They find what they want in printed material, on audio- or videotape, and more and more frequently on the Internet. Beginning in 1991 the Cleveland Public Library was the first large library in the country to provide Internet access to the public. We were, however, far from the last, as today 60 percent of public libraries provide information to the public through this important electronic medium.

But technologies continue to change, and what was once the exclusive domain of books, newspapers, and magazines is now shared by the Internet and will in the future be shared by digital broadcasting. Although many of us think of television as a distribution mechanism for entertainment, it has always had a larger public responsibility, as demonstrated by broadcasts of the Persian Gulf War, confirmation hearings of Justice Clarence Thomas, children's educational programming, and a recent tradition of televised presidential debates. Even the controversial broadcast of the O. J. Simpson trial served to stimulate widespread public discussion of race relations in the United States, a topic that has smoldered underground for far too long.

With the advent of digital television the public responsibilities of broadcasters will expand in direct proportion to expanded technical capabilities. As television moves beyond entertainment in a definitive way to transmit data and even provide an interactive capability now available through wired computer transmission, digital broadcasters must be a part of our long-standing national commitment to public access to knowledge and information, a commitment that gave rise to public schools, public libraries, and, most recently, public access to the Internet through libraries.

As technologies continue to change at an ever increasing rate, the public has come to rely on the library to ensure that information does not become the sole prerogative of the rich. In the poll referred to above, 81 percent of those interviewed said that "because of the increased use of computers and information technology, libraries are more important than they used to be." Far from becoming obsolete, libraries are becoming essential to the lives of the vast majority of individuals in the community.

Digital television is the next big leap in the development of information technology. Discussing the future of digital television today is like discussing the future of computers back in the 1970s when I opined that they would never have a significant impact because the storage capacity was too small. While it is true that the digital spectrum is limited, it is not yet clear what that limitation may mean in the future as signal compression technology improves. My best guess is that whatever any of us may anticipate today will fall far short of the reality. Still, many are suggesting that digital broadcasting will be the vehicle that brings the vast holdings of the Internet to the masses. If that is the case all of us have a stake in ensuring free public access to the information people need to live every aspect of their lives.

Whether future delivery systems are wired, wireless, or some combination of the two, there is a rich opportunity for public libraries to work with broadcasters to ensure public access to information. A dedicated, interactive "library channel," for instance, would enable anyone without a computer or an Internet connection to access the full range of electronic library offerings using his or her television. These offerings already include the Library's catalog, numerous electronic databases, access to other libraries, access to other Internet resources, materials that the Library has digitized, materials that other libraries (including the Library of Congress) have digitized, and educational programs (including computerized literacy training programs). At a time when only one household in seven has access to the Internet, this scenario is appealing for public as well as commercial ventures.

Commercial and public interests are not always at war. Often they exist side by side in a symbiotic, mutually productive relationship. One example of this is the now almost ancient relationship between libraries and bookstores. Study after study has demonstrated that people who use libraries also buy books; they don't use libraries instead of buying books. It is not a zero sum game. The existence of each encourages the use of both.

The United States has a long-term commitment to educating and informing its citizenry. And for good reason. Educated and informed people not only contribute to the community as a whole, but educated and informed people are also more likely to buy other goods and services; they are employable and interested in a broader spectrum of activities. Today there are many routes to the same truth. Libraries and educational institutions must be part of the broader picture. Use of the latest technology to further educate and inform citizens will be of benefit to our entire country—socially, politically, and even economically.

16

The Yin and Yang of Knowing

Information theorists and practitioners have announced the information revolution. They tell us that computer and communications technologies will transform every aspect of our lives, from the way we know what we know to how we choose to govern ourselves. They predict the overthrow of print as a communications medium in favor of digitized information, consumed screen by screen from a computer attached electronically to the Internet. They contend that libraries will vanish from the Earth, an anachronism in an electronic age.

There is no question that computer and communications technologies will play a role in our lives; they already do. The issue is whether the operative metaphor is the invention of the automobile, with its displacement of the horse and buggy, or something more akin to the invention of the television, a device that coexists with the radio, movies, and now videos as each fills a part of the information/entertainment spectrum. In short, will electronic technologies displace the printed page and revolutionize the way we make sense of the world, or will they work with existing ones, each occupying its own niche? Let us look at some of the basic questions.

Is It a Revolution?

The human spirit longs to live in revolutionary times, times loaded with meaning, pregnant with anticipation, full of promise for the future. Previous generations amplified their lives through religion, a system of belief that embodied social value and promised life everlasting to the true believer who followed certain rules. With the growing devaluation of religion, the need for value and hope has found its way into new systems of belief that many embrace with the intensity and commitment previously reserved for matters of divine revelation.

These new systems of belief are often cast as revolutions, since they predict massive change throughout society, but they are often based on a limited set of observations and have a bias toward a specific set of actions. Some examples: In the post-World War II era we believed that science would bring us peace, prosperity, and at least a modicum of stability. As a nation we pursued the secret of the atom and the challenge of walking on the moon. As the baby boomer generation came of age, sex replaced science, and we came to believe that "all you need is love." Grown up and disillusioned, the idealism of the flower

"The Yin and Yang of Knowing," reprinted by permission of *Dædalus,* Journal of the American Academy of Arts and Sciences, from the issue entitled "Books, Bricks, and Bytes," fall 1996, vol. 125, no. 4

children gave way to money as a measure of value, and many believed—or acted as if they believed—that "the one who dies with the most toys wins," a slogan based on the belief that winning was the goal and spending the way to achieve it.

Ironically, the most revolutionary development of the past fifty years in the United States was not seen as a revolution at the time. It became a revolution gradually, as millions of Americans changed the conditions of their lives. It was the suburbanization of America, a revolution that finds its roots in the invention of the automobile, the passage of the GI Bill, and the enactment of the Civil Rights Act. Flowing from the desire for home ownership, the forces of government subsidy, mobility, and empowerment led to a de facto caste society in which people sort themselves by race, ethnicity, and wealth. This, in turn, led to the current problems of isolation and urban decay, conditions that have created a vast underclass of people who are unable to participate in the information revolution because they are unable to read. It is hard to imagine electronic technologies transforming the lives of the 50 to 60 percent of urban public school students who fail to graduate, are unable to get and hold a job, and live on the margins of society. There may be a revolution here, but it is not an information revolution. If there is a transforming effect at all, it is among the educational elite.

For them, information theorists make extravagant promises of a perfect life in cyberspace, a new democracy where every man and woman can pursue his or her heart's desire in the pale glow of a computer, a virtual community where everyone has access to all recorded knowledge at the click of a mouse. New words have entered the language: Internet, World Wide Web, Netscape, user group. We surf the 'Net, travel the information highway, and interface with other like-minded souls.

Postmodernists like Sherry Turkle, professor of Sociology of Science at the Massachusetts Institute of Technology, claim that in this new, revolutionary information age "no unitary truth resides anywhere. There is only local knowledge, contingent and provisional. . . . The surface is what matters, to be explored by navigation. . . . Postmodernism celebrates this time, this place; and it celebrates adaptability, contingency, diversity, flexibility, sophistication, and relationships—with the self and with the community." Computers and the Internet, she claims, are postmodern because they foster "the precedence of surface over depth, of simulation over the real, of play over seriousness."[1] Or, to put it another way, nothing is true in or of itself; truth is only an artifact of social negotiation.

Other writers predict "the displacement of the page by the screen,"[2] and that "hypertext" will remove "the limitations of the printed page."[3] Turkle notes that "we've had a long run with print," and that "print has been a transparent medium for expressing a unitary self."[4] She believes that computers and computing networks are more in line with what she sees as a new, integrated reality.

These and other writers suggest that screens will replace books, that everyone will have access to everything electronically, and that the electronic media will significantly change—"revolutionize"—the way we know what we know and how we interact with each other on the basis of that knowledge. In short, they are predicting the death of books, the end of libraries, the abandonment of organized knowledge. Knowledge gives way to information and data—more data, faster data, information and data without bounds.

While these ideas are not really new (Marshall McLuhan concluded that the medium is the message more than twenty-five years ago, and Pierre Teilhard de Chardin was developing his theory of the Omega point in the 1940s), they do take on new meaning with the proliferation of personal computers and the enunciation of a national goal to wire America (first the United States, then the world). But are they revolutionary? If by revolution we mean a sudden, radical change affecting a large percentage of our society, the conclusion would have to be no, based on the alarming, and growing, portion of the population who cannot afford a computer and could not read the digitized text it they had one. If by revolution we mean a sudden, radical change in the way the rest of us get and use information, we must examine other questions.

Will Books Go the Way of the Horse and Buggy?

To understand the relationship between the printed and digitized word (or image) we must first understand the difference between knowledge and information. While information may be thought of as a simple data point, knowledge requires data collection, contemplation, and the integration of new principles into an existing fabric of knowledge. While information may be random and dissociated, knowledge requires organization of some type and implies value. Knowledge answers the basic question: What does it mean? A reporter, for instance, may announce that the war in Bosnia is heating up. From an epistemological perspective this statement already implies an understanding of the concepts of war and nationalism, but beyond this most basic organization the statement might be considered information. If the listener also knows where Bosnia is and something about its history, he or she adds the additional information about war to the preexisting base of knowledge, and his or her understanding is richer.

While it is clear that information and knowledge are interdependent, information tends to be more postmodern, to use the words of Turkle and others, while knowledge still has something of an old-fashioned flavor about it. While information may be contingent, knowledge requires context. Information may be fast; knowledge often comes more slowly.

Claims for the revolutionary nature of digitized information are often based on assumptions that everyone will have access to everything quickly and at a cost that is trivial. In fact, we are far from having all information digitized. Some experts estimate that less

than 1 percent of all information is now available digitally. Nor is everyone online. In the United States fewer than 10 percent of households have Internet access. Finally, while it is undeniable that cost to access and retrieve digitized information is falling and that the Internet is the most efficient way to get some information, it is also true that surfing the 'Net can become a very time-intensive and inefficient way to get other information.

If the claim that everyone will have access to everything quickly and efficiently is not now true, the question remains, if it were true, would it be desirable? From a practical perspective, does it make sense to invest the massive resources necessary to convert the remaining 99 percent of existing information into a digital format?

Some distinctions are in order. For very specific information, like the latest stock market quotations or a recipe for vegetable lasagna, there is nothing better than the Internet, especially with the graphic capability of the World Wide Web. Less precise questions may, however, yield hundreds or even thousands of sites of dubious origin that may or may not contain accurate information. For still other material, usually of a more conceptual nature like history, philosophy, or fiction, print may in fact be the most efficient delivery system. Books are still pretty handy packages, and people often behave in ways that are not strictly logical. Some may borrow a book from the library before deciding to buy it. Others, especially frequent travelers, may choose to purchase a paperback over a hard cover because of weight.

This bias toward print for some documents was acknowledged by Bill Gates in a recent speech at Harvard University.[5] Gates noted that even at Microsoft, when a document runs to three or four screens people tend to print it out rather than read and use it in a digitized format. This suggests that in some instances the Internet merely becomes a faster distribution system for what is still a conventional information package.

There are reasons people prefer print for some documents and a computer screen for others. A printed document is essentially different from an electronic one. Digital information is, as Turkle says, postmodern. It is present, contingent, two-dimensional, and value-free. On the screen everything has equal weight, equal value. Nothing is more or less important than anything else. And everything is fast. That means that information arrives quickly, it is (or can be) current, and users tend to bring a short attention span to the task, with behavior that is more like that of skipping from one television program to another than it is like that of reading a book.

Information that is better in digitized form includes items that benefit from the characteristics of the electronic media: speed in access, currency, and the ability to skip from screen to screen. Some examples of this type of information include: data (statistics, lists, stock market quotations, preliminary findings of ongoing research; anything that is immediate, changing, hard to keep up with in print, and does not require sustained thought), information specific to one person or institution (homepages that provide more localized information about individuals or institutions than would be economical to print and distribute widely), and articles now published in scholarly journals. An additional type of document that benefits from the ability of the electronic technology to multiply and enhance distribution is primary source material that is now unavailable to casual researchers or students because of the fragile nature of the material or the remoteness of the holdings.

There is a distinction between information that remains digital and is manipulated on the screen and documents that are simply transmitted digitally because of the speed and ease of distribution but are printed out at the receiving end and used as one would any printed document. In the first instance, information that changes quickly, such as a stock market quotation, is treated as something instant, contingent, of limited continuing usefulness. In the second instance, when documents like journal articles or primary source material are printed out, the Internet functions as a very large, omnipresent copying machine, and it is hard to maintain the preeminence of the screen over print.

If the bookshelves in the local bookstore or library are any indication, one might even argue that computer and communications technologies have done more to encourage conventional publishing than they have to replace it. *Wired*, a graphically flamboyant publication with an electronic sibling called *Hot Wired*, is a magazine devoted to the finer points of the electronic revolution. Although *Wired* is as hip and trendy as any magazine, it recently launched its own publishing company, *Hard Wired*, that will publish, surprisingly, books. Such important revolutionary gurus as Nicholas Negroponte, Bill Gates, and Sherry Turkle have also chosen a very old-fashioned format to carry the message of the revolution.

Why? It may be, as Nicholas Negroponte suggests, that the technology has not yet achieved enough market penetration to reach everyone that one wants to reach, but it may also be that books simply do something different. Negroponte himself hints at this when he explains: "Interactive multimedia leaves very little to the imagination. . . . By contrast, the written word sparks images and evokes metaphors that get much of their meaning from the reader's imagination and experiences. When you read a novel, much of the color, sound, and motion come from you."[6]

This is true, of course, but there is more to it. Books are different from digital documents, and for that reason they are unlikely to disappear. Books have substance. They take up space. They present us with a past, a present, and a future. As you read or thumb through them you are aware of how much has come before and how much is yet to be discovered. That in itself provides a context for the instant message, a frame that helps to understand where you are in relation to the material at hand. This context provides its own value system, its own set of assumptions and beliefs. You, the reader, are free to accept or reject those beliefs and values, but at least you know, or can know, what they are. In a hypertext world where you are propelled by your mouse from one screen to another, these contexts disappear, making it difficult for the reader (or viewer) to know if a term used in one document even means the same thing in another. While this is no problem with data, where we can make some assumptions about meaning, it may present difficulties in highly conceptual material like history, philosophy, and literature.

If digital information speeds things up, books slow things down. If digital information encourages us to get more information faster, books encourage us to linger awhile and contemplate what we have read, to think about the meaning of history or the beauty and subtlety of the language. If the electronic media revs us up by offering the world at our fingertips, books calm us down, encouraging us to think about what we have read, to understand what we have learned. There is more to knowledge, to life, than speed. Milan Kundera points out, "Speed is the form of ecstasy the technical revolution has bestowed on man."[7] He explains: "In existential mathematics, that experience takes the form of two basic equations: the degree of slowness is directly proportional to the intensity of memory; the degree of speed is directly proportional to the intensity of forgetting."[8] If Kundera is correct, digital information may give us more facts faster, but books help us become wiser.

What about Libraries?

Some maintain that the information revolution will make books and libraries obsolete. Others maintain that these new technologies will so transform libraries as to render them unrecognizable as the institution so many cherish. While technically and theoretically we can conceive of the entire Library of Congress on a compact disc the size of a quarter, the likelihood of such a development occur-

ring in the near future is remote. Reasons for this include the cost of conversion from print to digital storage, the bias toward print for documents longer than a few pages, the continued existence of legal impediments contained in copyright law, and the role of the library in providing context.

Although contemporary documents and other media are regularly produced digitally, conversion of existing documents is limited by the size and scope of the undertaking. To give one example, the Library of Congress has embarked on a program to digitize some of its one-hundred-million-item collection at the rate of roughly a million items a year. At that rate, if the Library adds nothing new, it will take one hundred years to complete the conversion and cost over a billion dollars. While costs will surely come down, and it is conceivable that libraries might jointly undertake such a project, one question remains: Should we?

The overwhelming preference for print has already been discussed. Additionally, libraries have some experience with this phenomenon. Some libraries, like the Cleveland Public Library, have been offering Internet access to the public for several years and have found that instead of replacing the conventional use of the library, electronic access (even to full text) has stimulated book borrowing, browsing, and use of printed reference material. It appears that electronic libraries not only provide information directly, but also advertise the existence of documents available in print and the vast store of resources in all media available at libraries individually and collectively. The fact is that with the dawn of the information age libraries are being used more than ever before.

The meaning of copyright in an electronic environment is cloudy. Publishers fear that if their titles were available online people would download a book in its entirety to read on the screen at their leisure. If the experience of libraries is any indication, it is more likely that the ability to browse electronically will stimulate, rather than replace, book sales. Most people would prefer to read a long document in print, and a printed book is a more convenient (and cheaper) package than a stack of paper printed at home or in an office. Nevertheless, fear of wholesale copying has led publishers to take a strong stand on copyright. They believe that the fair-use doctrine has no place on the Internet and that royalties should be paid for every electronic "hit." Issues of copyright in an electronic environment are complex and unlikely to be resolved anytime soon. Meanwhile, copyright is a much larger impediment to the electronic transmission of documents than technological or economic obstacles.

Libraries do many things. They collect, organize, and preserve; they make knowledge accessible—not books, but knowledge. Knowledge requires organization, context. Many argue that the Internet and the Web have created a new paradigm, that a new organization will emerge out of chaos, that systematic classification of knowledge is outmoded, and that Boolean search capabilities, hypertext, expert systems, and their offspring will revolutionize the way we think, the way we know. Yet the more there is on the Web, the harder it becomes to find. Even simple searches yield many hundreds of hits, many of them irrelevant. Microsoft, Sun Microsystems, and others are now developing indexing systems that seem like something out of *Star Wars*, although the structure is closer to Dewey or the Library of Congress classification schemes. If we assume that print and electronic information will coexist for the foreseeable future, it would make sense to use existing classification schemes and apply them to all types of information, print and digital alike, thereby facilitating the use of both in a complementary fashion.

If a book provides context for a document, a library provides context for all of human knowledge, knowledge that may be found in many documents and all types of information. If a book provides a sense of history of what came before and what is likely to come after the page being read, libraries provide a history of civilization. By their existence they imply that there is more to the study of philosophy than a book by Kant, more to the study of science than an article on geophysics, more to literature than the *Divine Comedy*. By their space and substance they provide a sensory understanding that knowledge is broader than any one subject field, that biography is related to history, that science owes much to mathematics.

It is this sensory understanding that we often forget when we discuss information. Humans are more than a collection of electrical impulses. Learning, knowing, takes place on many levels. There are things we know intellectually, and there are other things we know physically; there are times we know something both intellectually and physically. There is something we know about knowledge when we walk into a library that we do not know when we sit at a computer terminal.

It is not surprising that as some announce the death of libraries, citizens across the country and around the world are investing billions of dollars, pounds, marks, and francs in rebuilding major national and urban libraries. In the United States alone, cities like Los Angeles, San Francisco, Denver, Phoenix, San Antonio, Chicago, and Cleveland have built or are building libraries. Libraries have become a national obsession. Could it be that we intuitively recognize the need for context? Or perhaps the reason is simpler. Perhaps libraries are a symbol of upward mobility and represent the possibility of a future better than the past or the present. Or maybe the reason is simpler still. Maybe people need to be near one another, in a safe place, where they can pursue knowledge in the company of others. There are, no doubt, practical, economic, philosophical, and symbolic reasons for the public's commitment to libraries, and the evidence of that commitment is all around us.

For libraries there is no choice between providing documents in print and information on a screen; they must offer both. Together they are the yin and yang of knowing: the male and the female, the active and the passive, the dark and the light, the sun and the moon. Both are needed, with each occupying a special niche and performing the task it does best.

In a recent book entitled *Longitude*, Dava Sobel describes the centuries-long search for the discovery of a mechanism that would correctly measure longitude, the lines that run from pole to pole. Latitudes—the parallels that circle the Earth—were established by observing the apparent transit of the sun over the Earth, with the sun appearing to pass directly overhead at the equator and with the Tropic of Cancer and the Tropic of Capricorn marking the northern and southern limits of the sun's apparent transit over the course of the year. Sobel concludes: "Here lies the real, hard-core difference between latitude and longitude—beyond the superficial difference in line direction that any child can see: The zero-degree parallel of latitude is fixed by the laws of nature, while the zero-degree meridian of longitude shifts like the sands of time."[9]

To find our way in the contemporary world of knowledge, we need the latitude and the longitude, the yin and the yang, the book

and the screen. Digital information is not a revolution but a development, albeit a fast one, and information is only part of what it takes to achieve knowledge. In the end it is not the speed of the information or even the information itself that will give our lives meaning. It is still what we do with it that matters most.

NOTES

1. Sherry Turkle, quoted in Pamela McCorduck, "Sex, Lies, and Avatars," *Wired* (April 1996).

2. Sven Birkerts, *The Gutenberg Elegies* (Boston: Faber & Faber, 1994), 3.

3. Nicholas Negroponte, *Being Digital* (New York: Knopf, 1995), 165.

4. McCorduck, "Sex, Lies, and Avatars," 109.

5. Harvard Conference on the Internet and Society, Harvard University, Cambridge, Massachusetts, May 29, 1996.

6. Negroponte, *Being Digital*, 8.

7. Milan Kundera, *Slowness* (New York: HarperCollins, 1996), 2.

8. Ibid., 39.

9. Dava Sobel, *Longitude* (New York: Walker, 1995), 4.

PART VI

Literacy

Universal literacy is our greatest social challenge. Yes, I know about welfare, the homeless and the AIDS epidemic, but I persist in believing that if people could read, some of our other social problems would be much, much closer to solution. The following essay was originally delivered as a speech. I have included it here not because it suggests a definitive solution to the problem, but because it raises some important issues about what the library can and should do with regard to literacy training. In many ways it is conservative. It warns, for instance, that "libraries cannot single-handedly make up for the deficiencies of our public school system," and suggests that libraries have always been a "learning institution" that promotes individual achievement.

The article also contains information about a study conducted in Atlanta in the 1980s that documented the different ways libraries are used in urban and suburban parts of our service areas. This study has never been written for the professional press, and I have always believed that it ought to be replicated in other parts of the country to see if differences persist regardless of location. The findings of the study suggest that as a profession we ought to rethink our attitudes toward the appropriate size and location of branch libraries. It may be that the best "outreach" we can provide for poor, inner-city residents is a good, if small, branch library within walking distance.

Embedded in the essay is the primary question that any librarian must ask: What is the role of the public library? Other questions follow:

- How does this role relate to literacy training?
- What can libraries do to encourage reading?
- Should libraries actively engage in the teaching of reading?
- Can they avoid it?
- Are there better ways to explain what we do to the public?
- Are there better ways to encourage children to come to the library to get the help they need?

In this, as in other issues, identifying the problem does not necessarily suggest the solution. The challenge for libraries is to provide the literacy training they can while still remaining libraries. That equation may have a different outcome in different communities.

17

Libraries, Literacy, and the Future

I will raise some questions and make some observations in the following areas: (1) the problem of illiteracy, (2) what libraries can do to solve the problem, and (3) near-term and long-term goals.

The Illiteracy Problem

First, the problem. Illiteracy is bad and getting worse. It afflicts every part of our society. I do not plan today to document the dimensions of the problem because that has already been done. It is a problem with which you are all painfully familiar. So let us begin by simply agreeing that the problem exists. Moreover, the solution to the problem must be a shared responsibility. The problem is of such a magnitude that no single institution can solve it alone. Universal literacy is a universal responsibility. Individuals and institutions must work together, and these working relationships are likely to vary from community to community, depending on conditions and circumstances.

Still, even as we struggle to achieve it, literacy alone is insufficient. I guess I'm troubled by the notion that if we achieve literacy we've achieved enough. I realize that that's

Reprinted from *Stengthening the Literacy Network: Proceedings of a National Forum for State Libraries, May 20-22, 1990.* (Massachusetts Board of Library Commissioners, 1990)

the first step, but I think it's also important for us to remember that it's only the first step on a long staircase. We live in a country that someone recently described to me as exceedingly stupid. No more than five of our congressmen can name five countries in Africa. We live in a country where many of our schoolchildren cannot locate their states on a map of the United States. And our former president went to South America and toasted the wrong country. I sometimes fear that I will wake up one morning to find that Vanna White has been elected president. Literacy is something we should strive for, but I hope we don't stop there. Libraries never have stopped there and I don't expect that we will now.

What Libraries Can Do

So, what can libraries do? Well, we can't do everything. I know that's an unpopular notion because we like to think of ourselves as somehow able to address all the important issues. But libraries simply cannot single-handedly make up for the deficiencies of our public school system. Let me give you an example. In Cleveland the public library has an annual operating budget of $30 million. We can and do do a lot. The public school system has an annual operating budget of $430 million at its disposal. We can't with what we've got make up for the deficiencies of an institution funded at roughly fifteen times the library's level of support. Until we are funded at that level, and probably even then, we should not try to emulate the public school system.

What libraries can do is to build on past patterns of success. Instead of adopting a classroom approach to literacy training, libraries can build on the base of individual learning.

Libraries, after all, are learning institutions, not teaching institutions. People come to libraries for individual attention, to pursue personalized goals. From that perspective libraries know a lot about literacy training. In fact, I believe that libraries have spearheaded literacy training as we now think of it for the past hundred years in this country. Many of our efforts go unrecognized because we haven't called what we do literacy training. We've called it reader's advisory service. We've called it summer reading programs. We've called it just plain good librarianship. I'd like to give you a few examples.

Latchkey children. We did not know in Cleveland that serving latchkey children was a problem until I got a call last year from the *New York Times* asking me how we were handling it. I said I did not consider it a problem. We believe that libraries are supposed to help children with homework after school and assist them in finding something interesting to read. We think that it is the mission of the library to be one of the resources available to children. We choose to define it as our job.

There are other examples of services I consider literacy training that we do not normally define as such. I remember when I was working on a bookmobile in San Antonio, and a teenager came in with his friends one day. I overheard him say, "Talk to her, she knows all the good books." Was that literacy training? Probably. I remember working in Dallas and having children come in to a branch. In one instance an individual youngster's reading level improved three grades in about six weeks simply because we gave him books he thought were fun to read. Was that literacy training? Would he have dropped out of school without the library? You decide.

I remember a young girl coming into the library with her mother. The mother spoke no English, only French, German, and Spanish. The daughter wanted a book that would enable her mother to learn to speak English. Was that literacy training?

Not too long ago I was seated at the side of a distinguished gentleman in Cleveland. This man is the owner of one of the largest corporations in the city. During the dinner he turned to me and said, "You know, I couldn't speak English when I came to this country." He was an eastern European immigrant. He said, "My family couldn't speak English either. We learned it all at the library. I will always support the library for this reason."

And my final story is of an opera singer from a very poor family in little Italy in Cleveland who told me, "Oh yes, the library is wonderful. I used to come down every day after school and get opera scores, and I would listen to the records, and read the opera scores, and later I sang opera. I could never have done that without the library."

Wonderful testimonies, and I am sure each of you in this room could tell more such tales, stories of lives changed by the library. The question is, what does it have to do with literacy? Is this service, this training, the basis of literacy? I believe that it is. I believe that we have been doing the job for a very long time, but we have just called it something else. We have called it library service. It is a platform from which we can build.

But we haven't stopped with traditional services. There are other things, controversial things, that libraries do. We have comic books in the branches in Cleveland. We do not care what they read as long as they start reading. And videos. Let me tell you what we've discovered about videos. When we put videos in branches our circulation of children's books went up 25 percent. Do you know why? Because the parents were coming in more often and they brought their children with them. So videos—in a very strange and tangled fashion, the presence of them in our branches—has helped in literacy training. Other services. We provide meeting rooms for tutors; I think most libraries do that these days. It's part of the cooperation I mentioned earlier.

There are some things libraries might do differently. Let's talk about measurement. I believe that the way we measure service distorts our goal. Circulation is a good example of this distortion. Several years ago I conducted a study of branch library service in the Atlanta-Fulton Public Library. We made an amazing discovery. The ratio of walk-in use to the circulation of material varied considerably in different parts of the service area. In the suburban areas the ratio was four to one. That is, there were four books circulated for each person coming into the branch. In those branches closer to the central city the ratio was two to one. In the poor inner-city neighborhoods the ratio was one to one, and in some cases there were more people coming into the branch than there were materials circulated. Surprised at the finding, we wanted to know the cause. We discovered that in poor neighborhoods children were prohibited from bringing books home. Their parents could not afford to be responsible for replacing them if they were lost or damaged. What does this tell us? It's a simple message. Different people use libraries in different ways, but allocating resources on the basis of circulation alone discriminates against the poor and makes meaningful literacy training impossible.

Adapting Our Resources

The most important resource we allocate is the branch library itself. In Cleveland we have a branch library within walking distance of every resident. We are told that we have far too many branches. But the users of our branch libraries are overwhelmingly poor. Two thirds of the people who live in Cleveland have no access to automobile transportation. Children who use our libraries after school walk there. I wonder, do you think there is a relationship between the decline in literacy and the decline in public library funding? I bring this up here, now, to those of you representing state library agencies, because

you are in the business of evaluating performance and setting library development goals on a statewide basis. Is the public good always better served by developing new programs? Is it possible that in some instances basic library service, readily available, would be more effective? There are obviously no easy answers to these questions. As usual the right answer is, it depends. Community needs vary, and balance must be achieved.

In Cleveland we're developing a new approach to literacy training that fits in with our community. It wouldn't necessarily fit in with other communities. We have a very active literacy group in Cleveland, the Cleveland Literacy Coalition, and it involves lots and lots of groups working together. I serve on the executive board. We provide space for tutoring in our branch libraries. But there are some groups whose needs are not being met. Recently I met with our branch librarians to discuss new roles for the library. We wanted to design a project that would make a real contribution. We wanted to build on our strengths, our experiences. They told me that they felt we could make the greatest contribution among children. The program was put together, and we are trying to get it funded. We call it a dropout prevention program. It is geared to helping children in the third grade to fifth or sixth grade. Studies have shown repeatedly that it is at this age that children go from reading words to reading meaning. If the transition is made children are very likely to stay in school. If it is not they are very likely to drop out, or at least to drop behind.

Our librarians have observed that even though there are never enough tutors for adult illiterates, and the problem is massive and growing, there are a lot of groups working on that in Cleveland, and we support their efforts. But no one is really addressing the issue of the child who is failed by the school. Libraries know a lot about working with these groups, these children. Among other things we discovered a few years ago that if we work with the Cleveland Indians baseball team to advertise our summer reading program, we can attract boys to the program.

This is information we can work with and build on.

The program we are putting together will use computer-assisted literacy training programs in several of our branches. This will build on our experience with children, the idea that the library is a learning institution with specific attention given to the needs of the individual, and it exploits the "play" aspect of the technology. We use computer workstations for almost everything else in the world. Cleveland is very sophisticated in its use of technology and we see no reason why we shouldn't extend that to use by people learning to read at any level.

Several years ago, when I was still in Atlanta, the library sponsored a similar project. The branch head of a library in one of the poorest neighborhoods persuaded me to install computer learning stations as an experiment. The response was overwhelming. Every day after school the branch was flooded. We circulated almost no books out of that branch but the use and contribution to the community was astonishing. Children came in to use the computers. They brought their friends. While some children waited their turn on the computers they looked at books. They learned to read. Of course, the credit for the success of the project goes more to the branch librarian than to the equipment. It was she who recognized an opportunity and made it work.

Our Goals

Some final comments. New projects, yes, we need to try new things. But we need to support basic library services first. We need to build on the things we do well, the things that we can be successful at, and we've been successful at a lot of things. I'd urge you to resist the temptation to support the latest fad while neglecting the tried and true. I find that the older I get, the more I sound like my mother. I don't know if any of you have that problem. But I remember the 1960s, and I remember

social responsibility, and I remember outreach and the notion that we should stick small caches of books in every storefront and church basement. And we did, didn't we? We were nothing if not socially responsible. The question now is, was that really good library service? It's interesting. I have people say to me now, "Well, yes, but what kind of outreach do you have?" And I say that we have a branch, a full-fledged, fully stocked, professionally staffed branch where children can come after school, and their parents can come after work, within walking distance of every Cleveland resident. And that's our outreach. And what we need to do is concentrate on getting those branches where they need to be.

Don't let me mislead you; I'm not suggesting that this is the pattern in all cities and in all circumstances. It certainly is not. I think it is an appropriate pattern for poor inner-city residents. I think it is not appropriate for suburban residents, most of whom have access to automobile transportation and few of whom are illiterate. But I believe that the first line of defense in our war against illiteracy is the branch library. If the branch doesn't exist there is simply nothing you can do to improve the service.

Well, our challenge is formidable. We want to work toward a nation that is literate. Beyond that I would hope for a nation that is knowledgeable and even wise. In the final analysis I believe that almost everything we do in libraries contributes to literacy. I think bringing good books to children is literacy training. I think helping people read music and realize their dreams is literacy. I think much of what we do is literacy training. I believe we should continue to try new programs. You will encourage them. We will apply for the money. We will work together. I urge you, when you go to work with public libraries in your states to develop programs and approaches that can be implemented. But please do not forget that our first priority must be adequate funding for basic library services. It is within the context of strength that new initiatives are most likely to succeed.

PART VII

What "Global" Means for Libraries

The following article is far from definitive. Still, very little has been written about the global role of libraries in general and even less has been written about the global role of public libraries. It is a topic that somehow eludes us as we concentrate on maintaining our budgets and developing services at a local level. To some extent the Internet is changing all that. Many libraries now have homepages and are busy digitizing special collections that are not covered by copyright. Today the problem is not as much one of planning as it is one of execution. Important public policy questions persist even as the technology advances, making global sharing easier and more ubiquitous than ever. These questions include:

- Who should fund activities that make a library's resources easily available to people around the world?
- Is there a way to reward and encourage worldwide cooperation?
- How can we justify spending local revenue on global services?
- To what extent will international treaties and copyright legislation change the way libraries do business?
- Should libraries internationally be concerned about the plight of libraries in developing countries?
- To what extent does the growing globalization of the publishing industry affect libraries?

It is easy to become preoccupied with problems close to home, but as the world shrinks in almost every way, the future is global, even if we look only within our own communities, even if we look only at the publishers that supply us with the documents and other materials we purchase. The goal of strategic planning is to be aware of the forces that affect our institutions, and globalization is a dramatic and pervasive force.

18

Is There a Global Role for Metropolitan City Libraries?

Is there a global role for metropolitan city libraries? The answer to this question, as to most really important questions, is maybe. Where you stand on this issue depends on what type of library you sit in. I would argue, sitting as I do in a public library, that the public library's potential global role is enormous. But overall, the library profession has been relatively myopic about the potential contributions that could be made to knowledge and scholarship by linking large public libraries as part of the universal library.

The conference literature for the 1993 meeting of the International Federation of Library Associations and Institutions (IFLA) described the universal library as the expression of "the concept embodied in the IFLA Core Programs that all information, and the media that convey it, must be available on a global scale to all who wish or need to extend their knowledge. This implies that every field of knowledge should be available to everyone everywhere on the planet. Libraries must work so that the attainment of this goal is realized without any kind of discrimination. Libraries are universal both in not excluding any type of knowledge and in providing and accessing knowledge worldwide thanks to the increased cooperation made possible through the new technologies."

There is no question that information and communications technologies have now developed to the point where companies and nations compete in a global marketplace. The difference between success and failure in this environment can often be traced to the availability of world-class information. Computers are bigger (in terms of what they can hold), smaller (in size), faster, and cheaper than ever—and the trend continues. Satellites provide instant communications around the world and fiber optics provide the backbone for national and international transmission of graphs, charts, and photographs, as well as text.

In spite of IFLA's goal and the library profession's technological sophistication, planning for libraries throughout the world proceeds largely without the participation of even some of our largest public libraries. In the United States, for instance, only a few public libraries are connected to the Internet. Many people assume that public library service is limited primarily to children and adults interested in reading best-sellers. They believe that public library collections are of little use to scholars, and we have failed to provide the communications links that might prove this hypothesis untrue.

Cleveland Public Library joined the Internet in 1991. This communications link has enabled us to search the catalogs of other libraries for our patrons and makes it possible for others to search our catalog. In a typical

Reprinted from *American Libraries,* September 1994

month we experience approximately eight thousand searches through the Internet. These searches originate from academic libraries in Israel, Australia, Sweden, Norway, Italy, Spain, Austria, the Netherlands, the United Kingdom, Canada, and Japan.

This translates into increased international interlibrary loan activity. One recent list of material loaned to other libraries included the following: the University of Tokyo, Japan, requested *Les etats de Languedoc et l'edit de Beziers;* Statsbiblioteket Arhus, Denmark, requested *Standardbred Sires and Dams;* Universitat Autonoma de Barcelona, Spain, asked for *The Trial of Jesus of Nazareth;* Stockholm University, Sweden, requested *Vospominaniia i Pisma* by Alexander Siloti; and the State Library of South Africa requested *The New Schools of New Russia.*

One might argue that Cleveland Public Library is not typical. That is undoubtedly true. Our annual operating budget is $34 million— with about $8 million spent on materials—to serve a city of 500,000 people. Our collection includes almost two million titles, over ten thousand current journal subscriptions, and another six million items including microforms, photographs, manuscripts, and maps. We have extensive special collections in folklore and orientalia, and a photograph collection that is international in scope. We have the most comprehensive collection of research materials on chess and checkers in the world.

One might argue that Cleveland Public Library is not typical but it is, in fact, more typical than one might expect. Other public libraries in the United States have special collections that contain materials of international significance:

- Detroit Public Library maintains the National Automotive History Collection.
- The Free Library of Philadelphia has an extensive historical collection of children's literature from 1837 to the present, with children's books in sixty different languages.
- Denver Public Library's Western History Collection contains over 70,000 volumes plus 8,000 reels of Western newspapers, 500,000 negatives and prints of Western life, some 3,000 maps, and other material.
- The New York Public Library includes the Schomburg Center for Research in Black Culture, with research materials about black peoples throughout the world, and the Billy Rose Theatre Collection at Lincoln Center, with a comprehensive research collection of all types of materials on the performing arts.

In fact, most metropolitan public libraries contain specialized material, typically with unique holdings, about the history and geography of the area. Nor are international collections restricted to metropolitan city libraries in the United States:

- In France, the Bibliotheque municipale in Grenoble contains first editions of French authors such as Ronsard, du Bellay, Montaigne, Descartes, Molière, and Corneille; the Crozet Collection on Stendhal; the Rey Collection on Socialism; and the de Beylie Collection on Indochina.
- In Spain, the Biblioteca Central de la Diputacion de Barcelona contains, as one might expect, an extensive collection of works about Catalonia, Valencia, and Majorca.
- Birmingham Public Library in the United Kingdom houses a Shakespeare library with over 40,000 volumes in eighty-six languages.
- The Ervin Szabo Municipal Library in Budapest, Hungary, includes the Budapest Collection, the Social Science Collection, the Vambery Oriental Collection, and the Hungarian Political Pamphlet Collection (1711–1911) of more than 10,000 items.
- The Osaka Prefectural Nakanoshima Library, the oldest public library in Japan, includes the Sumitomo Collection of science and technology materials, the Matsushita Collection of electrical-

engineering materials, the Ishizaki Collection of Japanese and Chinese classics, the Sato Collection of Korean classics, and the Asahi-Shimbun Collection of Japanese classics.

- The Biblioteca Municipal Mario de Andrade in São Paulo, Brazil, includes extensive holdings of Brasiliana in the Felix Pacheco Collection.

In point of fact, the assumption that public library collections are limited and parochial is unfounded. There is a richness, a diversity, and even an eccentricity in these collections that make them every bit as valuable to scholarship and research as the collections of some of our academic institutions. Indeed, many of these public libraries have become the de facto library for nearby colleges and universities.

Delivering the Goods

But international cooperation depends on more than the quality of a library collection. It also requires the use of standard bibliographic data, access to holdings information, and the ability of a library to deliver the document once it is requested.

The development of international standards has been the subject of dialogue among national and research libraries for some time. Considerable success has been achieved in this area. But the extent to which large municipal libraries embrace these standards depends to a great extent on bibliographic cooperation and sharing within a country. A public library cannot depart from the customary practice of other libraries within its country. It must therefore rely on current practice.

Remote access to information about a collection depends on the degree to which a library has automated its catalog. In countries such as the United States, the United Kingdom, Germany, and Australia—where computerized catalogs are the norm and retrospective conversion makes the entire collection available—access is relatively easy. In places such as Italy, Greece, and eastern Europe, computerization of library catalogs is not widespread and access is relatively difficult. There are still many libraries in the world that rely on card catalogs.

Finally, the ability to deliver documents when requested and identified may depend more on staff availability than on any other factor. Since most of these materials are not available in an electronic format, their use rests on an individual library staff member who can either copy or mail the document. While this may be a trivial problem for the British Lending Library, it can be daunting to the National Library in Florence, a public library in which low pay has resulted in absenteeism that forces the library to open only on a sporadic basis.

Before we can come to grips with the question of cooperation among countries, we must address the level of cooperation *within* countries. Issues include the sophistication and development of national networking, the level of financial support for public libraries, and sentiments of nationalism.

Networking development within countries is uneven. In Europe, the richer northern countries have very well developed systems for library cooperation and these tend to include public libraries. The poorer southern countries tend to have literally no interlibrary cooperation of any type. Some countries, such as France and the United States, have tended to develop networking that relies primarily on academic research libraries and excludes large public institutions.

Libraryland's Poor Relations

That exclusion is a reflection of the overall level of support enjoyed by public libraries worldwide. For some reason, public libraries tend to be the poor relations of the library world. They are frequently excluded from national planning and left unfunded in areas that would make them full participants. This is true even in the United States, where libraries are relatively well supported.

Without adequate funding public libraries cannot take advantage of the opportunities made possible by technology—no matter how wonderful their collections may be. Many public libraries do not have the resources they need to purchase books, pay staff, or house either. For some it is a daily struggle to meet the most basic needs of the regular user. It is unreasonable to expect a library without enough money to open at regular hours to serve its citizens to commit resources that will enable a user halfway around the world to borrow from its collection.

The problem goes beyond the level of funding to the matter of source of revenue. How do you explain to taxpayers why their money is being used to serve someone in another city, much less another nation? International cooperation is only possible when there is some level of funding that comes from a larger political jurisdiction, such as a nation or a state.

One might even argue that public libraries really ought to be funded at a national level to enable them to share resources freely, even within the country. It is certainly no accident that Finland—a country that circulates an average of seventeen books per capita per year via 1,500 public libraries and eighteen thousand mobile-library stops, and provides more than thirty million books and one million recordings to a population of 4.9 million—supports its public libraries with both national and local monies. A broader funding base appears to be a fundamental ingredient for effective and efficient public library service even before we get to the issue of international cooperation. It is hard to imagine international cooperation with only a local budget.

Planning Away Protectionism

Nationalism is a final inhibiting factor to international cooperation. Significant differences in library size, language, culture, tradition, and political affinity create barriers that are difficult to identify and almost impossible to overcome. Each city, and each country, wants to control its library. The concept of resource sharing that is so obviously necessary

in an academic or research environment is far more difficult to explain to a city council or local electorate.

Perhaps more significantly, national information policies often determine whether information transfer between nations is easy or impossible. Economic protectionism sometimes expresses itself in out-and-out censorship of foreign publications or the barring of access to telephones, copying machines, and other communications technologies. Such protectionism can be destructive, as happened when Brazil prohibited the importation of computers in the 1980s to protect its domestic computer industry. This resulted in the crippling of other industries that were dependent on computer technologies to be globally competitive, and a consequent lag in research that put Brazil a generation behind in the development of information systems. While these issues may not seem specifically relevant to the international sharing of information among libraries, they establish the environment in which libraries, especially public libraries, must function.

International coordination and cooperation among libraries depend on the development of strong library networks, effective communications infrastructures, and common protocols that permit them to interact. The first step toward international cooperation between large public libraries is to achieve participation in library networking within the country. At present, development is uneven both in the progress of national networks and the participation of public libraries in them.

Communications infrastructures have taken different developmental paths in various countries. France, Germany, and Singapore rely on central planning, and each country has invested heavily to establish and maintain government-controlled communication systems. The United States and the United Kingdom have pursued the same goal by cultivating competition in both the telecommunications and information industries—although recent movement within the United States to establish a National Information Infrastructure appears to be a small step in the direction of centralized planning. Japan began with centralized planning and has moved toward a competitive environment. Although separate from library networks, these communications systems clearly condition the attitudes and options available to librarians developing national networks.

Road Construction Ahead

So far I have concentrated on what public libraries have to contribute, but highways carry traffic in both directions. It is not only a question of what we have to lend; it is also a question of what we need to borrow. The universal library concept articulated by IFLA refers to the availability of knowledge "to everyone . . . without any kind of discrimination." Again, there is the assumption that public library users have only the most basic information needs, that those with sophisticated questions go somewhere else to find answers. While I cannot speak with certainty about the use of all public libraries, I do know that in Cleveland our users are far more sophisticated than that.

By networking regionally, nationally, and internationally, public libraries can provide their local users with the information they need for work, for school, and to satisfy their personal desire to know more. Research for students at any level will be limited only by their level of interest. Individual citizens will be able to explore any topic in a depth currently available only to the educated elite.

The world is now engaged in developing technological superhighways that will link institutions, cities, and nations. The question I first posed may be answered another way. If we define global role as information and materials that contribute to the creation of knowledge and understanding, the answer is most assuredly yes. But if we define global role as inclusion in a substantive way in electronic networking, then the jury is still out. But to answer no will have dangerous social consequences. We may return forever to a time when only monks and scholars and those employing them will have access to the common bond of knowledge.

PART VIII

The Library of Congress

The Library of Congress is certainly the most important library in the country and arguably the most important library in the world. As such, what it is and does has an impact on all of us. This was the most difficult article I have written and I did, in fact, go through three complete rewrites. The debate over whether the library should belong to the Congress or the nation is old, the information massive, the politics internecine. It is a topic that is difficult to get your arms around, and change—given the law of bureaucratic inertia—is extremely unlikely. Because the library is so wonderful it is easy to overlook its unrealized potential. Because the library community, the Congress, and the Library of Congress have more pressing problems to solve, it is difficult to generate the level of intensity of concern that would raise this issue higher on the national agenda. Without that intensity, without that concern nothing will change.

In spite of the unlikeliness of change, the role of the Library of Congress is still worth discussing:

- What difference does it make whether the Library of Congress is designated a national library or not?
- What would be the advantages of change?
- What would be the disadvantages?
- What impact does technological change have on the debate?
- Why is the Library of Congress important to other libraries?
- Why is it important to the people of the United States?
- What do you see as the future of the Library of Congress?

19

More than a Library *for* Congress: Making LC the Nation's Library

No one browses the shelves of the Library of Congress (LC). They are closed, even to the staff. You have to know what you want, fill out a slip, and wait for someone with special clearance to bring the item to you. The process takes about ninety minutes for the first book—if it is on the shelf. You really have to want that book, and you have to be in Washington, in LC, to wait for it.

Technology wonks tell us all that is about to change. They promise that if we build the nationwide electronic superhighway they propose, a network of fiber-optic cable (which includes the National Research and Education Network, or NREN), we will all be able to browse the shelves of LC electronically, at the speed of light, from our homes, offices, or libraries. They promise us that we will have the entire intelligence of our species at our fingertips.

The promise is half true, because it addresses half the problem. The communications technology that will enable us to send massive amounts of data faster than you can read this sentence is available now, and a national program for planning and building the system is in place. There is not, however, a parallel program to convert portions of the LC collection to a digital format that could travel down the road. To extend the superhighway

analogy, you can't use a horse and buggy on the interstate.

The convergence of the growth of knowledge and the expansion of technology has created a moment of opportunity. It is now technically possible to put the holdings of LC within reach of the scholar and the schoolchild. As exciting as this may be, it is unlikely to happen as long as LC remains Congress's library. The subordination of LC has inhibited its ability to provide broader and more sophisticated information services to citizens and scholars. It has limited its ability to digitize the abundance of information in its possession, to participate as a full partner in national planning, and to work with writers, publishers, libraries, and scholars to resolve critical legal issues in the electronic transmission of information. Before LC can realize its potential as a twenty-first-century library, it must be designated and funded as a national library dedicated to serving the information needs of the citizens of the United States.

Why LC Is the Logical Hub

LC is not just the largest library in the world, it is the largest accumulation of knowledge in human history. With a collection of more than 100 million items, it surpasses the famed Alexandrian Library by more than a thousand times. It includes more than twenty million books in 470 languages, more than four million maps and atlases (some more than six centuries old), fourteen million prints and photographs, and more than 600,000 videotapes and films. LC contains the nation's memory and perhaps that of the entire world, as the Asian division contains more Chinese materials than any institution outside China and more Japanese materials than most institutions inside Japan.

This wealth of information is housed in Washington, D.C., just opposite the Capitol in three buildings containing 64.6 acres of space. These are the Thomas Jefferson building (1897), with a capacity of four to five million books; the John Adams building (1939) with ten to twelve million; and the James Madison building (1980), which is the largest federal building in existence except for the Federal Bureau of Investigation and the Pentagon. Already bursting at the seams, these buildings are supplemented by 350,000 square feet of secondary storage in Maryland and Ohio and under a mountain in Pennsylvania.

Some believe that our national library is not LC but an amalgam of all our nation's libraries. They argue that other libraries working together in a distributed network, like the ones provided by OCLC and the Research Libraries Group (RLG), can provide access to even more material than is available through LC. While it is true that the amount of information in all libraries across the country exceeds that of LC alone, the success of a national electronic library requires extensive coordination, communication, and leadership.

Others believe that new resources will be developed by the private sector. They claim that databases with the most up-to-date information will replace libraries as suppliers of data and documents. They point to the thousands of databases already available and their growing numbers. Most of these efforts, however, concentrate on current publications on scientific and technical subjects. While it may be true that a scientist doing DNA research may not need much in the way of historical material, the same cannot be said for the historian looking for information about primitive democratic societies. Database develop-

ment is in its heyday, but most commercial efforts begin with the present and concentrate, as one might expect, on those efforts likely to turn a profit. Database producers often ignore knowledge created before 1990 (or whenever they started producing their particular database) and leave subjects like literature, philosophy, arts, history, and social sciences by the wayside.

An effective national electronic library, one that will take maximum advantage of a sophisticated electronic communications system, will draw on the holdings of LC, other libraries across the nation, and the thousands of electronic databases that now exist or will be created. This can only happen if some institution provides the coordination needed to achieve cooperation among libraries; the leadership required to work with Congress, the National Science Foundation (NSF), and other agencies involved in the development of an electronic infrastructure; and a focal point for the resolution of copyright and other legal issues. Because of the size of its collection, its strategic location in Washington, its illustrious history of service to Congress, and its continuing struggle to serve researchers nationwide, LC is the logical hub for this developing electronic wheel.

The Problem with Congress

The question of who owns LC is not as arcane as it might sound. A longtime employee and observer of the library has summarized the problem succinctly: "For years we were trying to run a great library without anyone noticing." The anyone he was referring to was Congress. It is difficult to provide world-class service to a nation of 250 million people and to keep that feat hidden from the body that provides funding and oversight. Jealous of its prerogatives and reluctant to share its resources, Congress has blocked initiatives by the library that would have benefited the general public for the almost two centuries the library has been in existence. This has forced the library to smuggle in national programs under the guise of recovering costs or improving services to the Congress itself. The result is a predictable pastiche of programs with no firm commitment or direction, no clear understanding of a national responsibility.

This may have been tolerable when the library instituted a program of selling catalog cards instead of acknowledging up front that it was supporting cataloging for libraries around the country. It may have been excusable when Congress prohibited access to the library's computerized resources by nongovernmental institutions. It may have been understandable when information sharing referred to catalogs, indexes, and other sources of information about information. Today, it is no longer even practical to think of the library as anything less than a national resource, but Congress continues to run the library as its private domain.

The Cost of Serving Congress

LC appropriations for fiscal 1992 allocate $55,725,000 of its $322,228,000 budget for the operation of the Congressional Research Service (CRS) alone, or a little more than $100,000 a year for every Senator and Representative. This does not include funding for buying and cataloging material, nor does it include funding for the development of electronic databases. This compares with an average per capita allocation of $20 per year for users of public libraries nationwide and $350 per student at most academic institutions. The annual library budget at our nation's most prestigious universities that regularly conduct primary research falls in the $500 to $1,000 per student range, with Harvard University reaching the stratospheric level of $2,200 per student per year, the highest in the nation. None of these libraries have the benefit of a copyright law requiring the contribution of every item in copyright to their collections.

Congress controls appropriations for CRS. This revenue may not be moved or reallocated within the library for other projects, even if such projects would improve the overall service of the library and indirectly benefit Congress.

Funds for Electronic Conversion

LC has taken a few tentative steps in the direction of converting its materials to an electronic format, but funding constraints severely limit these efforts. The American Memory Project is an experiment that packages and distributes text, photographs, movies, and sound recordings about a specific subject on optical discs.

Selected libraries and a few schools are now evaluating these offerings. They have found that while these items provide an interesting educational tool that provokes curiosity among students, they are not particularly useful to the researcher or scholar seeking specific information. In spite of its limitations, this is the single most important conversion effort going on at LC. The budget for the project is $1 million a year, about the same amount of money needed to serve ten members of Congress.

Access to LC Resources

In other experiments, LC has begun to make selected databases available to the public on a limited basis. For years LC has maintained a database called SCORPIO (Subject-Content-Oriented-Retriever-for-Processing-Information-On-line) that provides legislative information including the legislative record, bibliographic citations on legislative topics, and complete text of Issue Briefs prepared by library staff summarizing the latest developments on topics before Congress. After repeated requests from libraries nationwide, LC began providing electronic access in 1993 to SCORPIO to people outside Washington. The library limits access to SCORPIO to sixty simultaneous users. There is local access in Washington from more than two thousand terminals. In the announcement the library noted that "service to congressional users would continue to be the library's primary goal for its online systems."

One-third of the library's immense collection is uncataloged and unavailable for use. Without a mechanism for finding materials there is no way to know what the library possesses. The nature of the materials left unprocessed (foreign-language print material, photographs, and other graphic information) suggests that Congress's unwillingness to appropriate funds or reallocate resources within the budget to solve the backlog problem may simply illustrate its lack of interest.

The LC Fee Initiative

Faced with the explicit charge to serve Congress and the implied responsibility to the nation, the library has struggled to explore opportunities offered by developing technologies without adequate funding. The library's response to the dilemma has been to seek legislation that would enable it to establish fees for specific services. These would include computer access to LC's collection. This proposal makes sense if we accept the notion that LC belongs to Congress and not to the American people. It is inconsistent with a broader mandate to support scholarship. Since electronic access will become the delivery mechanism of the future, the long-term result of establishing fees would be to inhibit the development of knowledge. The fee initiative flies in the face of the promise that every schoolchild and scholar will have LC online. Only those scholars and schoolchildren with a generous line of credit would have access to LC.

Conflicting purposes permeate LC, as the above policies illustrate. There is no evidence that change is possible as long as the library reports exclusively to members of Congress who make up the Joint Congressional Committee that functions as the library's Board of Trustees. The Smithsonian Institution and the National Library of Medicine (NLM) exemplify other approaches to governance that provide representation for a national constituency. The Smithsonian is a federally chartered, nonprofit corporation with a Board of Trustees composed of elected officials and private citizens. NLM is successful in providing the very latest information needed by physicians and medical researchers across the country largely because its independent board is made up of physicians and researchers.

Building a National Library

What would it take to make LC as effective in bringing information to the public at large as NLM is in meeting the information needs of the nation's medical community? The scope of knowledge is far larger and the potential constituency is far more diverse, but the goal is similar and the technologies are identical. The first step is to designate LC as our national library with specific, articulated responsibility to the nation. Second, Congress must provide for a governance structure that will enable the library to carry out its mission. Finally, it must be funded at an appropriate level.

As the national library, LC would develop a program to put its resources and the resources of other major libraries into the hands and minds of those needing them. It would use the existing and emerging electronic highways to deliver documents, maps, photographs—information in all its variety—to businesses, researchers, students, teachers, and the simply curious. This program would include the conversion of portions of the library's collection to electronic formats, the coordination of library participation in the program nationwide, the resolution of substantive copyright issues, and participation in the development of the electronic infrastructure.

The success of a twenty-first-century library and the test of its value to the nation depends on its ability not just to deliver information about documents but to deliver the documents themselves. Advances in computer and communications capacity now enable us to handle information in an electronic environment. Publishers routinely digitize books and magazines prior to or upon publication. Electronic databases now store information previously unavailable in any format. Nevertheless, most of the holdings of LC cannot be delivered electronically. For that dream to become a reality, 100 million items must be made electronically searchable, a costly and time-consuming task requiring the resolution of many sticky copyright issues. It will raise policy issues and change forever the relationships among authors, publishers, researchers, and libraries.

The creation of electronic versions of books, magazines, and documents will reduce the staggering storage requirements of the library and enable it to make effective use of off-site storage without diminishing access to needed materials. Once they are available electronically, these items can be retrieved using keyword searching capabilities, rendering cataloging as we know it obsolete, thereby eliminating the enormous backlog.

An expanded purpose and the technology to accomplish it are not enough in themselves. The challenge of making our nation's intelligence available to the nation requires more than even LC can do on its own. Equally important to the national agenda is a mechanism for encouraging greater cooperation and coordination among libraries across the country. This will require the library to engage in national planning, research and development, education, and grant-making activities. Planning is necessary to set a clear direction; research and development will invent or unveil the technology required to move in that direction; education will enable our nation's libraries to work together effectively from a base of shared expectations; and grants-in-aid programs will provide incentives for other institutions to participate.

The quickest way to convert print material to a machine-readable format is to share both the effort and the benefit from the effort. Consider as an example a program to convert back runs of magazines into a machine-readable format, a project far too costly for any one institution to take on and without the potential economic payoff necessary to attract commercial interest.

LC could establish standards and teach them nationwide. It could coordinate R&D efforts to ensure the use of the best and cheapest technology. Finally, it could encourage the participation of libraries in the conversion project by making grants to institutions agreeing to convert specific titles. Duplication would be avoided and distribution assured. The project would enable students, scholars, businesspeople, in fact anyone, to identify and download any article published at any time and stored physically in any library.

Reallocating Federal Library Aid

The Department of Education (DOE) administers grants-in-aid programs to school libraries, public libraries, and academic and research libraries. Money available for these programs is a piddling $147 million per year, and the library program is buried deep in the bowels of DOE bureaucracy—clearly not a departmental priority. As currently mandated, these funds support a broad array of programs that often satisfy purely local needs. Redirected, this funding could begin to build a cohesive and coordinated network in which the whole would most decidedly become greater than the sum of the parts. Mechanisms could be established that would ensure that even the smallest libraries would be connected to the emerging library network and incentives developed to stimulate the identification, preservation, conversion, and sharing of materials across political and institutional lines.

The recently introduced Electronic Library Act is a good example of a congressional attempt to achieve these goals within a confusing bureaucratic framework. Designed to develop state-based electronic libraries, the bill authorizes $10 million in FY94 and $25 million in FY95 to NSF, an agency that has had little experience with libraries but plays a major role in the development of NREN. A national library, already charged with achieving these goals and responsible for both grants-in-aid programs to libraries and coordination with NSF technical efforts, would be a far more effective home for this important effort.

When all of these systems are finally in place individuals will continue to obtain materials in frequent demand (children's books, best-sellers, basic reference materials, collections required to support specific research) at their local public, school, and academic libraries, but those libraries and their users could rely on the national network, with the national library at its hub, to meet more specialized needs.

Copyright protection was originally developed to protect writers, composers, and others who depended on their intellectual efforts to support themselves. The law was written when movable type was the most radical technology at hand. Its drafters never imagined a time when an entire encyclopedia could be copied onto a disc small enough to fit in a shirt pocket. They never imagined that an electronic network might transmit thirty thousand pages a second. They never imagined that researchers might be supported by academic institutions that in turn might stake a claim on their output. In short, those who fashioned the original copyright legislation never imagined today. While there have been rewrites and updates and revisions of that legislation, few would argue that it is adequate to meet today's needs. The resolution of intellectual property issues is central to the future of the electronic transmission of published information and will require the best thinking of writers, publishers, and librarians. What better place to address these issues head-on than at an LC, freshly empowered to work with all constituents for the national good?

New Governance for LC

To accomplish its ambitious mission, LC will need a governance structure that is accountable, flexible, and reflects its broadened mandate. It need not be a part of either the executive or legislative branches of the federal government but would be most effective as an independent entity like the Smithsonian. The Smithsonian board consists of members of Congress, the vice president of the United States, the chief justice of the Supreme Court, and private citizens. In the case of the library, citizen representatives should be selected from among well-known authors, scholars, librarians, and publishers.

As a national library, LC would continue to be tax-supported but also would be empowered to seek private grants and to enter into cooperative development agreements with private sector corporations. Monies already available could be spent more effectively by reallocating some of the CRS support to the development of electronic access capabilities and targeting grants-in-aid programs to develop a more cohesive approach to national library cooperation. One might also argue that part of the $2.9 billion already authorized for the development of the electronic delivery system might be allocated to developing the information to be sent over the system.

What's in It for Congress?

The U.S. Congress now enjoys the finest, most sophisticated library and information service on the face of the earth. Why would Congress give up this perquisite of power? Unquestionably, the nation as a whole benefits from actions of an informed legislative body, no matter what the cost. Is it reasonable to suggest that the system be changed in a way that would appear to penalize the Congress?

The answer is yes, and the reason is simple. Congress would not be penalized. In fact, Congress stands to be better served with direct electronic access to documents it needs. CRS is so costly in its current configuration because it relies on staff rather than systems to retrieve and analyze information. The transformation of LC from a nineteenth-century institution to a twenty-first-century library will enable CRS staff to serve Congress faster and more efficiently.

Members of Congress would also benefit from the impact of an electronic LC on voters. The tangible contribution to education, business, research, and personal discovery would be an innovation that could benefit every constituent in every district in the country.

We have reached a moment of opportunity. The flood of knowledge and the advancement of technology generate more information than we can comprehend and new ways and places in which to store it. LC is our greatest information resource, a legacy that has been passed down from generation to generation, a birthright that supports our democratic form of government. We have reached a moment when this venerable institution can become more than a museum, more than a warehouse, more than a library for Congress. We have the technology to put LC in the hands of every American, regardless of age, race, geographic location, or economic condition. We must seize this noble moment.

PART IX

Personal Style

Written almost twenty-five years ago, the following article is still very personal to me. I have often wondered to what extent interviewing five remarkable women influenced my own career development. Five women. Many things have changed since 1975. Today there are many more women in top administrative positions and women are far more mobile than they used to be. In fact, many women managing both large public libraries and large academic libraries today have served in more than one city, on more than one campus. Women today are frequently recruited along with men and compete on a much more level playing field. But the women interviewed for this article were pioneers, and as pioneers they still have something important to tell us.

I have included this article not for what it says about women, but for what it says about personal style. Then, and now, successful women and men "exhibit a high level of individuality. There is no need for this type of person to conform to any preconceived stereotype." They know who they are. Then, and now, they are strong, confident, and aggressive. Then, and now, they are sensitive to people, to politics, to nuances. Then, and now, they are "strong, determined, self-confident." They "work hard, think straight and have a fine sense of humor."

20

Five Women

Clara Jones

Dignity. If one were to describe Clara Jones in a single word, that word would have to be dignity. There are of course other qualities—strength certainly, courage, and a strong sense of commitment. But it is dignity that one remembers about Clara Jones.

Seated in her office, she spoke to me in quiet intense tones of her own history as a woman, as a black woman, as a female administrator. She spoke of the controversy surrounding her appointment in 1970 as the first woman and the first black to direct the Detroit Public Library, fifth largest in the country, and some of the reasons behind her recent successful race for the presidency of the American Library Association.

> Our social problems, which include cultural, educational and everything else, have been allowed to snowball to the point where we are desperately looking for remedies to a desperate situation. But we've been dealing with externals rather than the heart of what our problems are. For that reason I feel that no one small segment of society can make enough of an impression. The various professional organizations must join hands and join

forces, each doing what it can do best, but working very closely with other professions. This would work for legislation, too. I think there is strength in alliances.

I asked her about Shirley Chisholm's often quoted remark that she had suffered more discrimination as a female than as a black. "I think she was fooling herself," she responded. "No, you can't get past the blackness. That's the first thing that hits you."

It was, Jones feels, her blackness together with the unconventionality of her appointment (she had been at a middle-management level) that was responsible for the hostility she encountered when it became known that she was being seriously considered for her present job. She explained her decision to apply for the position at the request of a board member:

> I thought about it, and I decided that I would apply. I knew that there would be consternation but I was not expecting the flood tide of rage . . . the scorn and disdain. I really wasn't expecting that. I knew that it would not be easy . . . but I wrote my letter.

In spite of the initial reaction she believes that, "Once you're in something you're in for good." She described her own demeanor during that period.

> I decided that I wouldn't get down in the mud slinging with them because I'm not ac-

customed to doing that, and I was not trying to get the job that way. I didn't want it on those terms, and they had many more forces to use in that way than I had. And so I decided that I would not become argumentative. . .

When asked what she considers her greatest assets, Jones replied, "That I am black, that I am a black woman and that I have had the necessary experience. . . . In addition I am sensitive to the staff as human beings." Ironically, as she describes them, her liabilities are the same: "I was not able to move up the ladder and have not had experience in some administrative areas because I am a black woman."

In an article in *Illinois Libraries,* Clara Jones wrote, "The black woman meets today's challenges as the freest spirit in America." When asked to expand on this, she noted

We're too close to slavery and our men have never been allowed to have jobs that amounted to anything as far as earning enough money to take care of their families. Nearly all black women have always worked. So it's no big thing in the black community for women to work. . . . Therefore the men have never been able to develop this kind of theory, "You stay in your place because I'm bringing the bread home and you do what I say." There's much more of a democratic spirit in a black family than there is in the middle-class white family.

"The slave woman" simply because she was a woman could sometimes defy power in certain situations. Sometimes she could save a life. . . . So she's always had that horrible responsibility, that extra little bit of power.

"I have never had any fetters on me," she continued, "about what I wanted to do. The only fetters were racial fetters."

Women have had a position of equality and power and recognition and they knew their worth. They haven't had to search their souls to find out if they are equal to a man. . . . It was a living thing. A black woman's every action was evidence of the necessity of her in-

put. Black women have a freedom of spirit because of that.

The family continues to be important to Clara Jones. She does receive help and support from her family; she has experienced no conflict between rearing three children and pursuing an active career that extends far into community involvement. "The mother community," she feels, "is as important as the mother in the home."

When asked about personal models, Jones listed a number of well-known, respected people, including black leaders of both sexes. More important, however, are "the individuals who are nameless as far as the world is concerned . . . charming human beings who have influenced me, intelligent black women."

Clara Jones is very much an individual, strong, confident, and comfortable with herself. In her own words, "I take my own outlook and I'm not afraid to stand up and say it."

Barbara Ringer

Competence and professional expertise are the characteristics one usually hears used to describe Barbara Ringer, register of copyrights at the Library of Congress. What is not spoken of quite so frequently is the underlying reason for this competence—her commitment to individual freedom and creativity.

In her own way Barbara Ringer is a renegade, an anomaly within the established order. It was she who challenged the Library of Congress when she was not appointed to her present position. She brought suit on grounds of racial and sexual discrimination, and she won.

In describing the way in which the confrontation developed she explained: "I have no doubt that the fact that I was a woman and that I was expected to be a good girl and shut up and not become an active candidate for the position had a lot to do with this [the ensuing conflict]. And there was very active and open discrimination against me not getting the job, but when the job was posted I applied."

She was denied the position, however, and subsequently filed an administrative complaint and brought legal action charging "patterns of racial and sexual discrimination at the Library of Congress." In the face of overwhelming odds ("My lawyer at one point said he thought I had about a 30 to 1 chance of winning on the racial and about a 300 to 1 on the sexual"), she persisted through a series of exhaustive and expensive hearings and appeals.

"I had no intention whatsoever of dropping the case and I was going to follow through—as far as I had to go, but I had no confidence that anything would come of my efforts. . . . I never had that much expectation of getting the job. What I was doing was not aimed at getting the job so much as not giving in to what I felt was a real honest-to-god injustice. And I felt I owed it to the people here—not just here (Copyright Office) but at the Library of Congress—to not drop it but to go on with it and I did have the resources to do this."

This unfailing determination to carry on what must have seemed like a quixotic battle was based on the same personal philosophy that has made her outstanding in the position of register of copyrights.

"I have a certain lifestyle which I guess carries over into my work. The two are co-extensive I suppose—which is based on my genuine belief in the reality of authorship—individual, creative, free authorship and the desire to promote that."

This same commitment to individuality and creative freedom is further manifested in the choice of people she admires. "I like women who believe in themselves," she responded to my question about possible models.

"I like people with guts. I'll give you some examples off the top of my head, people who certainly I have no intention of modeling my life after but who just give me a little lift when I think about the fact that they told the establishment to go sit on a tack. Maria Callas is one—a thoroughly selfish woman, great artist who knew what she wanted and went after it. Muhammad Ali who is a very very

different type of person just stuck to his guns. . . . I'm willing to take my models where I find them but they're not models in terms of women who have made it."

It seems appropriate that a person whose job it is to protect the creative product of individuals should feel so strongly about individual freedoms.

A single woman and a lawyer, Ringer feels that her greatest liability has been "discrimination against women." "I would have had an entirely different kind of career if I had been a man." At the same time she feels her greatest asset has been her "professional knowledge" gained working twenty-six years in the Copyright Office. Many would agree.

In spite of her expertise, however, she had some questions about her ability to function effectively as register after the extended litigation. These fears were quickly dispelled.

"After all was said and done I was rewarded in my belief that librarians are the salt of the earth and that basically given the opportunity to behave well they will when others may not. I have had little or no trouble. The library administration has been more than just gracious, but genuinely cooperative.

"There have been no recriminations against me despite this fairly sharp confrontation that I had with the library administration."

In summarizing her experience Ringer also summarizes something about herself: "There were quite opposite assumptions. One was that the only reason I went into this was that I wanted the job. That wasn't true. At the same time I did want the job, not because it would make me happy (and I was right) but because I felt in the broader sense of the term it was about the only thing I could do and live with myself."

Lillian Bradshaw

Open, "affirmatively aggressive," eager to explore new ideas. Lillian Bradshaw belongs in Dallas, where Texans rest secure in the belief that theirs is the best of all possible places. Though a native of Maryland, she is a true Texan by choice and as proud of the place as she is of the Dallas Public Library, which she directs.

Outspoken and straightforward as one might expect, Bradshaw spoke in familiar Texas accents of her satisfaction with public librarianship and with Dallas. "What I've wanted to do is be a damn good public librarian and run a good public library system for a city that I happen to like very much because it's been very kind to me. I'm working in a city that's growing and changing very rapidly and it has been really great to work with people whose ideas are expanding, the population is expanding . . . a city that supports library service."

Married with no children, she attributes her professional achievements to "a personal peace with my private life so I have time and energy to devote to my professional life."

As outstanding as her career has been with a term as president of ALA and one of two women suggested as a potential Librarian of Congress, it has not been without difficulty, even crisis. "The day I was to be confirmed as library director of this library a councilman rose and said that he could not vote for me to be library director because there were books in the library that should be taken off the shelves. The Council did not vote. It was a difficult decision. I don't think I really ever doubted what my answer would be. I made the decision that I had the freedom to be a professional librarian out of respect for the Dallas citizens who had the right to read what they wanted to read or I did not want the job. The next week I was confirmed 8 to 1. It was a very difficult week for me but it was something I could not condone and would not condone."

This experience is undoubtedly one of the reasons she feels so strongly about attempts at censorship and describes her models as those people who defend intellectual freedom.

"I most admire the librarians who during the McCarthy era stuck up for academic freedom and intellectual freedom and the freedom to read. I think that took a hell of a lot of guts. And I'm afraid if they hadn't done it then we would have had more trouble right now than we're having. Bill Dix is one of the ones who was on the front line of that fire."

Responding to a question about discrimination, Bradshaw recounted an event that occurred shortly after her appointment. She was told that she "needn't bother to come to the department heads' meetings because they were only of interest to men." She attended, of course, and notes that now "They know better than to discuss libraries without Bradshaw on board."

Her relationship with the other department heads is now a pleasant and productive one without strain or difficulty, and her effectiveness is easily demonstrated by the growth of the Dallas Public Library. Moreover she commented "I like men. . . . I love being the only female department head."

Bradshaw feels that her greatest assets are that she "chose public libraries" as her area of interest and that she had a "well disciplined library school experience at Drexel." In addition she notes, "I like people." Her liabilities she feels are that she has little patience and expects too much too fast: "I want the world."

Sherrie Bergman

Sherrie Bergman is young. She is also small, articulate, and ambitious. She is one of a new breed. Director of the Wheaton College Library and former director of the Roger Williams College Library, she is, at age twenty-nine, one of the youngest, if not *the* youngest, director of an academic library in the country.

A native New Yorker, Bergman grew up in Stuyvesantown, a "white middle class suburb in the middle of Manhattan." As a younger woman, it never occurred to her that she wouldn't have a career, and her career has been meteoric, but in a different way than she had originally planned. "I have not always thought of myself as being in an administrative position and certainly never at such a young age. . . . Having been successful at one step made me realize that I could be much more careful about what I would select as my next step."

Bergman is divorced, mobile, and frank about her ambitions. She sees her greatest asset as her experience performing library tasks at every level and her willingness to admit there are things she doesn't know.

"Nothing replaces the experience of going in and doing everything from the ground up. This is one reason why there are so many women today who would make excellent administrators. They have actually gone up the ladder, beginning with learning how to file catalog cards and how to sort punched McBee cards at the circulation desk. Most men have gone from library school to become directors and assistant directors. They really have no concept of what some of the day-to-day problems are on the job because they've never gone through any of this. There are a lot of women who are in dead-end positions who have had just the kind of experience that can make them very sensitive and very understanding about a lot of those problems on the job. They probably will be less prone to making unfair demands."

As "that little girl who is running the library," Bergman has encountered some predictable difficulties and has had a certain amount of on-the-job assertiveness training: "One problem I had in adjusting to administration was learning what I should be asking for, not just for myself but for my staff, and going out and fighting for it." Bergman feels that women are traditionally uncomfortable making demands: "Too many of us were raised to feel that whatever we did with our lives, our role would be secondary."

This is frequently manifested in a reluctance to discuss salaries: "Women are extremely uncomfortable about talking about money, partially because very often the woman is not the chief breadwinner in her home. This is not as true today as it used to be. But many times women started to work to supplement their husband's income. Today the divorce rate being what it is and with the woman usually being the one who has custody of the children, times have changed. But a lot of it still holds over and women are often taught that it's not polite to talk about money."

Bergman feels that the answer is a "professional consciousness raising." Her own consciousness seems already to be raised in spite of the fact that she feels her greatest liability is that she is not hard enough on herself.

Bergman has not yet faced the career crises which mark the development of the other women nor has she achieved the record of years of successful accomplishment that they have. She has, however, confronted the problems of youth and issues arising from her position as a young female administrator. She is articulate and has the intelligence and self-confidence necessary to deal with the inevitable conflicts and changes when they come.

Margaret Chisholm

Poised, articulate, ever in control, Margaret Chisholm clearly knows what she's about.

Previously dean of the University of Maryland's College of Library and Information Science, she was recently appointed vice president for University Relations and Development at the University of Washington, making her the first woman vice president in the 114-year history of that institution. When asked why she was appointed to her new position, Margaret Chisholm replied with cool self-confidence, "Because I'm good. I've had appropriate experience."

With her knowledge and experience it's hard to believe that she received her library degree as recently as 1958 when she returned to school, the mother of two children. Ambitious and determined, she worked, continued in school, and received her Ph.D. in 1966. "I started late but I started fast."

Her own struggle for education accompanied by a variety of jobs has led her to some very definite conclusions about employment: "I think that anybody who's willing to work can get a job. I've worked at packing apples, clerked in stores. Things have not been easy, but I've always had a job. Sometimes they paid ten cents an hour, but I've always worked. So I just think that anyone who's willing to work hard can find something to do."

When asked to speculate on the difficulties of the female library administrator she observed: "You can't have this dichotomy between women and men. . . . I don't really see it. There are certain characteristics that a leader has and I don't think you can define it by man or woman. . . .

"There has been discrimination. I can't say that there hasn't been discrimination. However, I just am not aware that that many women have sought to be directors of academic libraries or directors of large city libraries. These are positions that take a lot of work and a lot of long hours. . . . I say yes, there has been some discrimination, but women are not without blame, because when they really wanted those jobs and really aggressively sought them, there are instances where appointments have been made. . . . it is not totally discrimination."

Her own success she feels is a result of "a tremendous amount of energy . . . optimism . . . and enthusiasm. I don't think there has ever been a time in my life when I told anybody that I'm too busy to do something. Everything that I've done," she noted, "seems to merge together and every experience builds on another. Any writing I've done, any research I've done, I've always been able to use in another way. It all builds. . . . Within a reasonable 18-hour day you can fit an awful lot.

"When I started as a librarian I was an elementary librarian in a school, and if anyone had asked me then I would have said, 'I will enjoy being an elementary school librarian for the rest of my life.' I was never able to project success, nor did I try to plan or figure for it. I would never have believed it in the first place. The fact that I ever got out of Gradyville, Minnesota, was a surprise to me."

She did, of course, get out of Gradyville, Minnesota, and has come a long way since then. Talking with Chisholm in her already abandoned office at the University of Maryland, my overriding impression was that this woman lives life totally and intensely. She laughs easily and seems to look for balance, humor, the fun in life. I got the feeling that she looks for perspective, and takes things seriously, but not herself.

SUCCEEDING IN THE LIBRARY FIELD

How do you get to the top in the library field? Do you really have to be a man—or a "tough broad"? Statistics and popular mythology suggest that this is the case. Studies have repeatedly shown that in a profession that is 84 percent female, the administrative level clearly remains a male bastion. A recent well-publicized survey of large public libraries in the United States and Canada revealed: 40 percent of the chief librarians are female in libraries serving a population of 100,000 to 400,000; 20 percent of the chief librarians are female in libraries serving a population of 400,000 to 750,000; and only 10 percent of the chief librarians are female if the population is over 750,000.

Nevertheless, there are women administrators, women who have made great contributions and achieved extraordinary success. Who are these women; what qualities, if any, do they share?

My investigation was an informal one. I interviewed five women chosen in an unscientific, arbitrary, somewhat eclectic manner. I sought diversity of age, type of library, geographic location, and career pattern.

Each of these women was extraordinarily generous with her time. Each talked with me at great length and was very frank in answering the many questions that I posed. As the interviews progressed I began to detect striking similarities among their diverse characteristics. Each possesses great inner strength and a strong sense of self-identity. While no personality "type" emerged, it soon became obvious that a successful woman, and probably a successful man, exhibits a high level of individuality. There is no need for this type of person to conform to any preconceived stereotype. In the words of Clara Jones, one must, "Create the reality and let the image take care of itself."

Femaleness

A strong sense of "femaleness" was present in each of the women. As Clara Jones put it so well, "With the degree of emancipation that has come to women now, they must not get in there and try to out male the males, or just to go in those same patterns that males are going in. I'm not talking about softness. I'm also not talking about hardness. Women come in and have to out men these men. And they aren't being good women and they're making out poor as men. So they get to be kind of a nothing."

Successful women, apparently, have come to terms with themselves not only as administrators but also as individuals and as women. Barbara Ringer expressed much the same sentiment.

"To put myself forward as a tough broad is not very profitable. I'm not a tough broad, although I'm going to be regarded as one until I prove otherwise."

While there is a firm belief that, in the words of Barbara Ringer, "A woman is absolutely the equal of a man as an administrator, not better, not worse, the equal," there is also a growing conviction that a woman has something very distinctive to offer as an administrator.

Margaret Chisholm notes "An administrator has to be able to make decisions rapidly, assess situations and at least understand as many sides of a problem as you possibly can and then be able to use sound judgment in making a decision. The other characteristic that may be more a characteristic of women than men is patience."

Lillian Bradshaw describes three particular areas in which she feels a woman manager excels: "A woman manager who has had good training and good sense to apply to her job also can bring sensitivity, open mindedness and a political astuteness to that position."

Clara Jones takes this even further. "Women," she feels, "have been allowed to care and express caring. And when you say caring you're talking about people. And when you're making policy at whatever level you're talk-

ing about people." It is this ability to go out of oneself that she finds lacking in our present social institutions. Women can "look more at issues" and "bring them (men) back to the heart of the matter." Relatively free from the ego hang-ups that Jones feels influence the decisions of many men, women have not only the ability but the responsibility to rehumanize our institutions. "Men have been running this world," Jones commented, "and look where it is. It's in pretty much of a mess."

Sherrie Bergman expressed a similar view when asked to speculate on the role of the female administrator. "The reasons for acquiring these characteristics are inherent in sexism in society, but the result is that 50 percent of our population would be more effective in positions of authority because they've been trained to think about the other side, whether at the dinner table or when it is necessary to accept the possibility that their view may not be the only one."

Why Library Sexism?

The fact remains, however, that the skills of 50 percent of our population are not utilized in this way. I asked the interviewees to comment on sexism within the library field and speculate on some of the reasons for it.

While there seems to be general agreement among the women with whom I spoke that sexual discrimination is a fact of life, there were several opinions as to the reason for this sad state of affairs. Barbara Ringer suggested that, "these patterns become so familiar that nobody can see anything wrong with them." Lillian Bradshaw, in elaborating on this concept, explained: "Because many management positions are occupied by men it is traditional for them to think that way. Only women's aggressiveness is going to change that." Bradshaw further commented, however, that "Women have only themselves to blame if they don't go after those jobs. Nobody's going to hand them one."

Margaret Chisholm, too, feels that "Women have not been aggressive in acquiring the background experience for that kind of position. . . . This means a tremendous amount of work which most women are unable or unwilling to do.

The first and most significant hurdle, it seems, for women interested in library administration, occurs with the selection process. Whether the predominance of the selection of males as chief librarians is a result of the "old boy network" as Sherrie Bergman and Barbara Ringer suggest, lack of preparation and aggressiveness noted by Chisholm and Bradshaw, or simply lack of interest on the part of a significant number of females, the fact remains that such positions are less accessible to women.

Women Have to Be There

While it is admittedly dangerous to make generalizations from such a small group, it is worth noting that four of the five women with whom I spoke had some relationship with their present employers prior to their appointments. Margaret Chisholm graduated from the University of Washington. Barbara Ringer worked for the Copyright Office for twenty-six years, and both Clara Jones and Lillian Bradshaw were on the staffs of their respective libraries when their appointments were made.

Both Jones and Bradshaw commented on this phenomenon. Each feels that she would have had very little opportunity to obtain her respective job if she had not been present. In the words of Ms. Bradshaw, "Both Mrs. Jones and I were on the staff. If I had been outside the staff of the Dallas Public Library, I'm not sure my application would have gotten the time of day. If I had not been here to push . . . I don't think I ever would have gotten an interview."

Women's Work . . .

Once appointed, there is a general consensus that women tend to work much harder just to prove themselves. As Barbara Ringer explains, "All you have to do is prove yourself and then you're home free, but you have to prove yourself over and over again as you encounter new people." In Lillian Bradshaw's

words, "A woman probably will work twice as hard to prove herself." Margaret Chisholm puts it in slightly different terms. Asked to tell the secret of her success she said, "I never say no. I have never turned down an opportunity." Her motto, she says, is "The harder I work the luckier I get."

When asked to comment on problems arising from male subordinates or peer relationships the responses were surprisingly similar. While a few isolated incidents were recalled, the universal response was "This is simply not a problem." Sherrie Bergman explained: "The boss is to be respected because that person occupies that position. It doesn't matter what form or what package that person comes in."

Being Part of the Place

An argument frequently raised to explain the paucity of female administrators is the traditional lack of mobility found among married women. "If a woman is interested in advancing her career," Sherrie Bergman explained, "she has to think very seriously about how important geographic location is to her. There is no question that I could never have achieved the success that I've had in my career if I had stayed in New York."

At the same time traditional patterns are changing. Not only are there increasing numbers of single and divorced women, but family structures are changing to accommodate career moves for women as well. Bergman noted from a recent women's conference that "Husbands and wives are now beginning to alternate as to whose career is going to set the next geographic location and which one is then going to tag along and try to find another job in that city or will they agree to try to live on one income for awhile."

Another aspect of the mobility issue that bears further examination is what I call geographic identification. If we are to theorize that each person has a place in which he or she is most himself or herself, it would follow that an individual would be a more effective administrator in that place than in another.

While I am not sure from my limited investigation how much importance to attribute to such a theory, it does seem to be an element in the lives of successful people, men as well as women. It seems, in fact, to be a natural extension of a strong personal identity and does carry over into an administrative style. Lillian Bradshaw expressed it well when she said, "Somewhere along the line to achieve your professional goal your style has to adapt to that city. I don't see how you could administer in a city that is contrary to your own characteristics."

No one familiar with Clara Jones and Lillian Bradshaw would confuse the distinctive styles of these two remarkable women. Each is strong, competent, and effective in her own city. It would, however, be unthinkable for them to change places and retain that effectiveness.

There are of course many qualities, experiences, and acts of God that contribute to a successful career. I asked what qualities had been most significant for each of the women. As might be expected, professional competence was mentioned frequently. Bergman explained in personal terms: "I try to be honest with myself about what I don't know and then try to gain that knowledge."

Openness and determination were mentioned repeatedly. Jones: "It never occurs to me that I can't do what I'm supposed to do. There is no such word as can't." Bradshaw: "Every chance you get you've got to take advantage of it. . . . You've got to be alert to things happening around you." Chisholm: "I have never turned down an opportunity. I'm never too busy. I have a tremendous amount of energy and have been highly enthusiastic about any job that I've had."

The five women attributed their success to many characteristics that I expected, but there were a few surprises. Successful women are indeed intelligent, articulate, and professionally aggressive. These qualities are not, however, developed by copying a "masculine" or even a "neuter" style. Women who achieve have strength and confidence in themselves. They know who they are, and they know they are women. But they do not confuse femaleness with softness and are willing to assert themselves and their abilities.

Not only are they comfortable with their femaleness but they see distinctive contributions which can be made better by a female than by a male administrator. Because of continuing discrimination encountered by women applying for high-level positions, women tend to work harder after appointments in an effort to prove themselves. Moreover, women are more sensitive to the individual needs of those who work for them.

I was surprised by the importance of geographic identity to success in view of frequent discussions about mobility as a necessary element in career advancement. Successful individuals, it seems, are comfortable not only with themselves, but with their environment as well. Whether a person chooses a place because he or she is comfortable in it or adapts a personal style to fit a local situation, a high degree of compatibility is apparent. A study should be conducted to explore the relationship between place and administrative style.

In the final analysis, what did I find? I found people. I found strong, determined, self-confident women who work hard, think straight, and have a fine sense of humor. I found a few individuals at least who believe in what they are doing and do it well.

There is no pat formula. Each woman must create her own career defined by her own ambitions and based on professional competence and personal security. Individuality is the key if indeed there is a key.

Clara Jones learned that lesson early from a loving grandfather who counseled, "I want you to always remember who you are."

PART X

Measuring Success

Statistics, service measures, whatever we choose to call them—a discussion of the tools we use to measure success in libraries is likely to induce sleep in almost any audience. While businesses use sales or profit figures to demonstrate performance and compare it from year to year and from company to company, libraries and other public sector institutions seem almost embarrassed by the need to talk about performance at all. As a result we continue to report statistics that no longer reflect what we do. Academic libraries compare the size of their collections and public libraries report circulation. While it is true that all libraries collect and report many different statistics, it is still these two, collection and circulation, that provide the snapshot of performance in the academic and public press; it is these two that are the default statistics that demonstrate use. Given the outmoded nature of our reporting, it is no wonder that the publics we serve fail to understand the sweeping changes that have occurred in the institutions we want them to support.

A pundit once said: you are what you measure. Counting, measuring, statistical reporting, all provide us with a way to talk about our institutions. They give us a context and a vocabulary for communicating purpose and performance. When we fail to count electronic access and count only documents held by an institution, we are ignoring the huge investment libraries have collectively made in a worldwide electronic infrastructure. This, in spite of the fact that electronic journals online are quicker to access and easier to use. Failure to count access as well as ownership also makes it more difficult to make internal management decisions, to evaluate the relative costs and benefits of one type of service over another. The fact that a subscription to a print journal is fixed while the use of electronic journals may be variable does not, by itself, make one purchase more favorable than the other.

Public libraries tend to be less concerned with collection and more concerned with usage. Given this, circulation became the key data point when most of our materials circulated. We all acknowledged that it was an imperfect measure but believed that it was the best available. City libraries argued that children in poor neighborhoods used materials in the library while children in middle-class neighborhoods checked theirs out and used them at home. Still, we measured and the press reported circulation. Today as inner-city residents use computers in libraries instead of using their own computers at home, the problem is exacerbated. And the problem is growing as circulations decline because it is easier to print out the full text of an article and take it home to keep than it is to check out the magazine in question and return it at a later date.

In a 1998 poll voters in Cleveland were asked: "Because of the increased use of computers and information technology, do you think that libraries are more important or less important than they used to be?" A surprising 81 percent responded that they believe libraries are more important. A look at some little-reported statistics shows why this is the case. When looking at total usage of the library (a number that included circulation, reference service, and electronic transactions) we discovered that usage had tripled in five years. *Tripled.* Nothing in the history of library service compares to the impact of electronic information services, and we are not reporting it regularly and in a systematic way to the public. This phenomenon is not unique to Cleveland. Libraries across the country could demonstrate similar astonishing changes in service and in public expectation of libraries. Still, reporters ask and we respond to questions about public library usage with circulation statistics.

There are lots of reasons this happens. Measurement of electronic usage is difficult. Many question whether we should count sessions or searches. We do not yet have the hang of reporting electronic usage in a way that is as intuitive and understandable as a simple circulation statistic. But consider what is happening. Students and others now come into our libraries and search our electronic catalog for books, they search the databases we subscribe to for articles, they search electronic encyclopedias, and they browse the Web. Sometimes they don't come in at all; they dial us up from home. These are real services; they are core services; they require the assistance of staff and an investment in technology; they take more and more of our resources and enable us to provide increasingly better service. If we don't count them and report them, we are preserving the fiction that libraries exist only to circulate books.

By counting both access and ownership to assess the size of a collection and by counting both electronic transactions and circulation of material for usage we do more than provide an accurate snapshot of what we do. We also provide a way to look at the interaction between electronic and more traditional services. Does circulation go down as electronic usage goes up? The answer is "not necessarily." Many library users seem to use print and electronic information interactively. Do students and researchers at a university prefer to do research in the stacks or online? My guess is that some use one, some use the other, and many use both, but in a more targeted way.

Electronic usage statistics today are imperfect, but data collection will improve. Even now, however, with imperfect statistics, we are doing our libraries and their users a disservice by not reporting more accurately how libraries are really being used. More important than the perfection of the statistics is our understanding of the strategic importance of measuring success.

Strategic management is not only about guiding individual libraries from today into the future, it is also about guiding libraries as a group into the future. If we don't know what we are trying to do there is no way we will ever know if we succeed. An immediate challenge for today is for library professionals to work together to redefine the terms "collection" and "usage." These terms must be used consistently for all libraries or they will lose their meaning altogether, but to continue to define them as we have for hundreds of years will cripple our ability to move forward. What we measure defines who we are—and what we will become.

Index

A

ability-to-pay principle, 71
access
    equity of, 24, 26
    to information, 23, 26, 38, 39, 100
    to international libraries, 117
    to the Internet, 90, 103
    as public good, 80
allocative efficiency, 73
Alvey Programme (United Kingdom), 11
American Memory Project, 123
artificial intelligence, 10
Association of American Publishers, 27
Association of Research Libraries, 97
automation, 65, 85-89
    effect on in-house use, 89
    of international libraries, 117
    legal issues, 87-88

B

Balanced Budget and Emergency Deficit Control Act (Gramm-Rudman), 8, 14
Beasley, Ken, 31
Beatty, Sam, 52
Bell, Daniel, 45, 78
benefit received principle, 71, 73, 79
Bennis, Warren, 4
Bergman, Sherrie, 132-33, 135
Bete, Channing, 37
Biblioteca Central de la Diputacion de Barcelona, 116
Biblioteca Municipal Mario de Andrade, 117
Bibliotheque municipale, 116

Birmingham Public Library (United Kingdom), 116
Board of Trustees, 56-57
books, 22, 25, 103-105
    bestsellers, 80
    circulation of, 22, 25, 112
    future of, 103-105
Brademas, John, 48
Bradshaw, Lillian, 131-32, 135, 136, 137
branch libraries, 19, 24, 112-13, 138-39
Brooks, Jack, 46
"Brown Bill," 51-52
Brown, George, 49, 51, 53
Bryce, James, 69
bureaucracy, 34, 48
Bureaucratic Inertia, Law of, 48

C

cable (transmission), 10
cataloging, 93-94
censorship, 92
change, 2, 8-15
    economic, 11-12
    political, 13-14
    social, 12-13
    technological, 9-11
    See also innovation
Chapman and Hall (publisher), 97
children
    latchkey, 111
    and literacy, 112
Chisholm, Margaret, 133-34, 135-36, 137
Chisholm, Shirley, 129

circulation, 22, 25, 112, 138-39
citizens' lobby, 40-41
civil service, 58
Clarke, Arthur, 43
Cleveland Public Library
    automation, 85-87, 89
    branches, 112-13
    and fees, 88
    and the Internet, 115-16
    literacy training at, 111
comic books (and literacy), 111
communicating, 4, 66
communications, 9-10, 45, 115
    costs, 10
    future of, 18
    history of, 44, 45
    information infrastructure, 18-19, 24
    and interlibrary loan, 18
    international infrastructures, 118-19
Communications Decency Act, 90
competition, 17
computers, 6, 9, 16, 44
    fifth-generation, 10
    silicon chip, 44
    See also technology
Congress, 122-23, 126
Congressional Research Service (CRS), 123,
    126
cooperation (library)
    international, 115-19
    politics of, 31-36, 51
    Regional Councils of Government, 32-36
    See also interlibrary loan
copyright (of electronic resources), 26-27, 66,
    87-88, 105-106, 126
Cory, John, 35
Council on International Communications and
    Information, 52
Council on Library Resources (CLR), 27
currency (of information), 18

D
de Tocqueville, Alexis, 77
demographics
    family, 19
    urban, 32
Denver Public Library, 116
    Librarians Committee, 35
Department of Education (DOE), 125

Detroit Public Library, 116
Dialog, 10
director (public library), functions of, 56-57, 62
discrimination, sexual, 135
document delivery
    international, 117
    from the Library of Congress, 124
Domestic Council Committee on the Right of
    Privacy, 45
Drennan, Henry, 35, 36
dropout prevention program (Cleveland), 112

E
economics, 68-82
    ability-to-pay principle, 71
    benefit received principle, 71, 73
    private goods, 71
    public goods, 70, 79, 80
    spillover effects, 71, 79
economy
    change in, 11-12
    international, 6, 12
elected officials, 60-61
Electronic Archiving (OCLC), 95
Electronic Collections Online (OCLC), 95
Electronic Information Delivery Online System
    (EIDOS), 11
Electronic Library Act, 125
Elsevier (publisher), 97
empowerment (of employees), 66-67
English, Glenn, 51, 52
Enoch Pratt Public Library, 35
equity
    of access, 24, 26
    tax, 71, 73, 75
Ervin Szabo Municipal Library, 116
European Strategic Programme for Research
    in Information Technology (ESPRIT), 11
externality (spillover), 71, 79

F
fee-based research services, 20-22, 24-25
    See also user fees
Finkler, Norman, 32
FirstSearch (OCLC), 95-96
funding, 57, 81
    grants-in-aid, 14, 125
    and international library cooperation,
        117-18

G

Galvin, Tom, 52
Garceau, Oliver, 80-81
Gates, Bill, 103, 104
Georgia Tech, 18
government expenditures, (table) 70
    local, 69-70, (table) 72
Gramm-Rudman-Hollings amendment, 8, 14
grants-in-aid, 14, 125
gross national product, (table) 70

H

Hard Wired (company), 104
HighWire Press, 97
Hofstadter, Douglas R., 28, 43
Hot Wired (magazine), 104

I

illiteracy. *See* literacy
Illiterate America, 8
implementation (of plans), 4-5
Individual Influence, Law of, 49
information
    access to, 23, 26, 38, 39, 100
    digital, 104, 105
    gap, 38-39, 102
    government role, 46-47
    infrastructure, 18-19, 24
    vs. knowledge, 103
    library provision of, 17-18, 23
    organization of, 25-26
    policy, 29, 45-47, 51-53
    politics of, 37-41
    print, 103-105
    and productivity, 46
    revolution, 101-103
    society, 78-79
    sources of, 13
    specialists, 22, 25
    technology, 14-15, 38, 42-47, 49
    value of, 46
Information Industry Association, 46
Information Needs of Urban Residents (1973), 35, 78
Information Science and Technology Act (1981), 51
innovation, 63-67
    partnerships, 65-66
    rules for, 66-67

    technological, 65
    See also change
Institute for Information Policy and Research, 49, 51
Integrated Searching (OCLC), 95
integration (of management functions), 5
intellectual freedom, 91
interlibrary loan, 18
    international, 116
    and OCLC, 94
    See also cooperation (library)
International Communications Reorganization Act (1981), 51, 52
international cooperation, 115-19
    document delivery, 117
    funding for 117-18
    and nationalism, 118-19
    standards for, 117
International Data Corporation, 9
International Federation of Library Associations and Institutions (IFLA), 115
International Thomson Organisation, 11
Internet, 99
    access to, 90, 103
    organization of, 26

J

Javits, Jacob, 48
Jones, Clara, 129-30, 134, 135, 136, 137

K

Kilgour, Fred, 11, 94
Kinder, Lorelei, 49
knowledge, 102, 106
    vs. information, 103
Knowledge Information Processing Systems (KIPS), 11
Kozol, Jonathan, 8, 13
Kundera, Milan, 105

L

Lang, Norton, 32
laser disk technology, 9
latchkey children, 111
law (pertaining to library automation), 87-88
leadership, 3
libraries, 79, 106
    automation, 65, 85-89, 117
    Boards of Trustees, 56-57

libraries (*continued*)
  branches, 19, 24, 112-13
  budgets, 57
  and change, 14-15
  and communications, 18
  and competition, 17
  cooperation, 31-36, 51
  as electronic publishers, 26
  fee-based research services, 20-22, 24-25
  funding, 57, 81
  future of, 16-22, 23-27, 105
  and information provision, 17-18, 23
  international cooperation, 115-19
  and literacy, 110-13
  metropolitan, 115-19
  mission of, 25, 26, 37, 66
  policies, 56-57
  and the press, 58-60
  and Regional Councils of Government,
    32-36
  regionalism, 33
  revenue, 71, 73, (table) 74, 78
  role of, 17, 37-38, 65, 67, 99-100
  suburban, 32
  and technology, 14-15, 17, 65, 67
  usage, 78
Library and Information Science Research
  Agenda, 53-54
Library of Congress, 20-27
  access to, 123-24
  collection, 121-22
  and commercial databases, 122
  and Congress, 122-23, 126
  document delivery, 124
  electronic conversion of collection, 105,
    123, 125
  governance, 126
  as national library, 124-25
  and technology, 121
  user fees, 124
Library Services and Construction Act, 36, 51
licensing fees, 88
listening, 4
literacy, 6, 8, 13, 15, 108-113
  training, 111-13
local government expenditures, 69-70,
  (table) 72
local revenue, 71, 73, (table) 74, 78
localism, 32

Longitude (book), 107
lumber yard approach, 53-54

M

Machlup, Fritz, 45
Madison, James, 37
Magnuson, Warren, 48
management
  leadership *vs.*, 3
  of personnel, 58
  and politics, 55-62
  strategic, 1, 3-5
  tactical, 1, 3
marginal cost, 75
Marshall, Mary, 35
Mason, Robert M., 18
Maximum Convergence, Law of, 49
McGovern, George, 48
McLuhan, Marshall, 102
measurement, 27, 112, 138-40
  of electronic usage, 139
Microelectronics and Computer Technology
  Corporation (MCC), 11
Mintzberg, Henry, 2
mission, 25, 26, 37, 66

N

National Information Infrastructure, 118-19
National Library and Information Services and
  Construction Act, 48
National Library of Medicine (NLM), 124
National Technical Information Service (NTIS),
  46
National Telecommunications and Information
  Agency, 45
nationalism, 118-19
negotiation, 61-62
Negroponte, Nicholas, 104
New York Public Library, 116

O

OCLC, 11-12, 93-98
  and electronic publishing, 96-98
  history of, 93-94
  mission, 98
  reference service, 94-95
Office of Management and Budget (OMB), 46
Ohio College Library Center. *See* OCLC
Ohio University, 94

online databases, 9, 80
    communications charges, 10
    licensing fees, 88
Online Journal of Current Clinical Trials, 97
organization (of information), 25-26
Osaka Prefectural Nakanoshima Library,
    116-17
outreach, 113

P
Paperwork Reduction Act (1980), 46
partnerships (with electronic publishers), 65
personnel management, 58
Philadelphia, Free Library of, 116
planning, strategic, 2-3, 4, 9
Plato, 16
Political Expediency, Law of, 49
politics, 28-62
    1980 election, 48
    change in, 13-14
    of cooperation, 31-36
    impact of technology, 42-47
    of information, 37-41
    and negotiation, 61-62
    politicians, 34-35
Porat, Marc, 45
pornography (on the Internet), 90-92
post-industrial society, 45, 78
power
    of Boards of Trustees, 56
    political, 28, 31, 36
preservation, electronic, 26
press (media), 58-60
    library spokesperson, 59-60
pricing, 88
    See also user fees
print resources, 103-105
prisoner's dilemma model, 50
private goods, 71
public goods, 70, 79, 80
publishing, electronic, 96-98
    libraries and, 26

R
Reagan, Ronald, 8, 48
reference services (and OCLC), 94-95
Regional Councils of Government, 32-36
    and library cooperatives, 35
regionalism, 33

research, 49, 53-54
    fee-based services, 20-22, 24-25
*Research Design for Library Cooperative Planning
    and Action in the Metropolitan Area,* 36
Resnikoff, Howard, 44
revenue
    and international library cooperation, 118
    local, 71, 73, (table) 74, 78
Ringer, Barbara, 130-31, 135, 136
risks (with technology), 67
Roberts, Larry, 8
robotics, 10
Roland, Jon, 38
Rutherford, Jim, 50-51

S
satellite dishes, 10
Sayre, Edward, 35
SCORPIO (Subject-Content-Oriented-
    Retriever-for-Processing-Information-On-
    line), 123
Scorpion System (OCLC), 96
selection policies, 91
service, levels of, 19-20, 24
sexism (in library field), 135
silicon chip, 44
Smithsonian Institution, 124, 126
Sobel, Dava, 107
society
    change in , 12-13
    post-industrial, 45, 78
South, Jean Anne, 34
spillover, 71, 79
standards (for international cooperation), 117
Steinmuller, Edward, 43
strategic management
    defined, 1
    functions of, 3-5
strategic planning, 2-3, 4, 9
suburbanization, 32, 102

T
tactical management
    defined, 1
    functions of, 3
taxation, 71, 73, 75
    efficiency, 73
    equity, 71
    property, 73

TBG (company), 11
technology, 9-11, 83-107
    automation, 85-89
    effect on print resources, 103-105
    information, 14-15, 38, 42-47, 49
    and innovation, 65
    laser disk, 9
    libraries, impact on, 14-15, 17, 65
    and the Library of Congress, 121
    and reference, 93-98
    role of libraries, 67
Teilhard de Chardin, Pierre, 102
television, digital, 100
Thompson, Frank, 48
Toffler, Alvin, 45
training, 27
trends, 6-27
Turkle, Sherry, 102, 104

U
unions (labor), 58
user fees, 69-76, 77-81, 88
    at the Library of Congress, 124
        options, 80
        See also fee-based research services; pricing

V
Vagianos, Louis, 31
vendors (commercial), 11-12
videos (and literacy), 111
vision, 3-4, 66

W
Washington, D.C., Public Library, 35
Weinberger, Casper, 49
White House Conference on Library and
        Information Services (1979), 37-41
Willard, Bob, 52
Williams, Martha, 95
Wilson, Ian H., 3
Wired (magazine), 104
Wirth, Timothy, 8
women, 128-37
World Area Radio Conference (1979), 47
WorldCat, 94
Wright, Jim, 8

Marilyn Gell Mason has been director of the
Cleveland Public Library since 1986. Previously she served as director of the Atlanta
Public Library and executive director of the
first White House Conference on Library and
Information Services in 1978. She is a frequent speaker and contributor to the professional press on management and policy issues. Mason currently serves on the boards of
OCLC and the Council on Library and Information Resources and is a member of the
IFLA Standing Committee on Public Libraries.